Qualitative Phenomenological Analysis of

IT Project Management

In Pharmaceutical Industry

Phil Ly

A Dissertation Presented in Partial Fulfillment of the Requirements

for the Degree Doctoral of Management in

Organizational Leadership and Information Systems

University of Phoenix

February 2013

Qualitative Phenomenological Analysis of

IT Project Management

In Pharmaceutical Industry

Phil Ly

University of Phoenix

Approved:

Stephen Ball, Ph.D., Mentor

Liston Bailey, Ph.D., Committee Member

Yongmin Zhu, Ed.D., Committee Member

Abstract

The purpose of this study was to analyze why IT projects continue to fail at a high rate in the pharmaceutical industry. IT projects failures delayed development of new drugs that can help save lives. It was imperative to understand why projects fail because it is a matter of life or death. This qualitative phenomenological study included analysis of which stage did projects usually fail and why by interviewing stakeholders, project managers, and project team members who had lived, first-hand experiences of IT projects in the pharmaceutical industry. A general anticipated outcome was a better understanding of what are leading root causes of IT project failures. Researcher completed data analysis phase using the nVivo 10 software and applied interpretative phenomenological analysis to develop interpretations and draw conclusions. The findings indicated that projects failed in six phases of a project life cycle. Paper contained several recommendations to address failure areas in IT projects in the pharmaceutical industry. Faster delivery of IT projects correlated to faster launch of new drugs to market that could save lives and aid in curing major health ailments.

Dedication

I dedicate this study to God, the Almighty, that through him we can accomplish all things. I am fortunate that he has given me the brain power, energy, money, and persistency to drive this journey to conclusion.

I dedicate this doctoral journey to my wonderful wife, Huong Nhu Le, for her financial, moral, and caring support through the years. I would have not started this journey without her persuasion and would definitely not finish without her insistent.

I dedicate this doctoral journey to my two princess-angels, Sophia An Ly and Jasmine Binh Ly, for their constant reminder of why I am pursuing this doctorate and why I do anything for that matter: to be a good father and role model to them. They have spent many weekends without dad's active participation in fun events the last few years. I promise I will make it up to them in many ways.

I dedicate this study to my two mothers, Hanh Thi Nguyen and Phan Thi Huynh Nga, for constantly reminding me the value of education.

Out of respect, I dedicate this study to my two late fathers, Phuoc Cong Ly and Hien Trung Le, for teaching me the responsibility of being an adult male.

I dedicate this study to Tai Nguyen, Hung Nguyen, and Tuan Nguyen for stepping in as father-figures.

I dedicate this study to my grandparents, Dinh Ngoc Nguyen and Nhan thi Nguyen who raised me during my childhood.

Acknowledgements

I acknowledge my strong dissertation committee for leading me through this journey. I am grateful for their assistance despite their busy schedules. I acknowledge Dr. Stephen Ball for mentoring and motivating me to temporary give up sleep and using his good sense of humor along with great knowledge of dissertation expectations. I acknowledge Dr. Liston Bailey and Dr. Yongmin Zhu for their valuable feedbacks and insights. I acknowledge the University of Phoenix doctorate program for being an outstanding institution. I acknowledge my extended family at work for understanding and supporting my pursuit of this doctorate degree.

Table of Contents

Table of Figures

List of Tables

Chapter 1: Qualitative Phenomenological Analysis of IT Project Management In Pharmaceutical Industry

The hospitals' quality of care, neighborhood pharmacies providing drugs, and people's livelihoods were at stake when there were delays in drug launches (Hsieh, 2009). Information technology project management failures caused billions of dollars in damages for pharmaceutical companies and delayed drug product launch for millions of patients (PMI, 2009). In 2007, the Standish Group reported IT projects success rate were only at 35% (Cerpa & Verner, 2009). In 2011, project success was up slightly to 37% ("Failure rates finally drop," 2011). Even without delay, a single drug required on average 12 years and $1.3 Billion to take a drug to market ("Project zero," 2009). Managing IT projects was a complex process (Wurst & Guernsey, 2006).

A project was a unique product or service designed to achieve a specific deliverable within a certain time frame with commitment of staff and resources (Nwachukwu, 2010). In short, a project was achieving a goal with a start date and end date (PMI, 2009). A project was also defined as a sequence of events and processes to fulfill an objective (Nwachukwu, 2010). An information technology (IT) project involved enhancements or changes in features to computer hardware, software, network, and other IT related infrastructure (Damaré, 2008).

The point was projects were continuing to fail at a high rate. Every project was dependent on an information technology component (PMI, 2008). The purpose of this study was to analyze why IT projects in the pharmaceutical industry continue to fail, so knowledge workers can take corrective actions to enhance success potential. Human lives were literally at stake. The failures of key IT projects could lead to the delay of the pharmaceutical organization's next major drug release or distribution, and thus can cause financial harm to the organization (Tobbell, 2009). For example, an Enterprise Resource Planning (ERP) software project failure forced FoxMeyer Corp, a drug company, to file for bankruptcy protection because the software to run its manufacturing system did not work (Scott & Vessey, 2002). The NHS IT Project to link major health and pharmaceutical companies with their patients went through $20 Billion before the United Kingdom's health minister canceled the project (Hough, 2011). Clearly, failed IT projects had a crippling effect on an organization's financial health.

The current study examined the perceived effects of how project managers directed the activities of a project from project start-up, planning, implementation, testing, and closure. Further examination included how project managers ran status meetings, updated management, and interacted within a matrix organization. In addition to studying the project manager's skills, the current study contained examinations of the experiences of project managers and organizational theories such (a) Frederick Taylor's scientific management theory, (b) Vroom-Yetton Jago decision model, (c) Rogers' diffusion of innovation theory, (d) Henri Fayol's management theory, and (e) Douglas McGregor's theory X and Y (Weiyin, Thong, Chasalow, & Dhillon, 2011).

This researcher used qualitative phenomenological study to explore the central phenomenon of why IT projects fail in pharmaceutical industry. Qualitative studies did not contain focus on measurements and statistics (Leedy & Ormrod, 2010). A phenomenological study included an analysis on people's perspectives of why they thought the IT projects failed (Willis, 2007).

This researcher conducted this study at Research Triangle Park, North Carolina. Research Triangle Park was home to more than 500 biotechnology, pharmaceutical and life sciences companies while employing almost 60,000 employees (Carolina Chamber of Commerce, 2012). The state of North Carolina consistently ranked as one of the top five states for pharmaceutical drug development in the United States (Carolina Chamber of Commerce, 2012). Conveniently, Research Triangle Park was also home to this researcher, so most pharmaceutical corporations were within 30-minute driving distance for the interviews.

Why Choose Qualitative Approach over Quantitative for this Research

Qualitative research was more effective than quantitative research in this study for many reasons. Qualitative studies were usually follow-ups to quantitative studies (Neuman, 2006). Qualitative research included description of events in the natural settings, and the intent of this study was to understand participants in their natural work environments (Willis, 2007). Also qualitative research contained analysis of a situation specific to a group (Neuman, 2006).

Researchers conducted many quantitative studies, and results shown that projects failed. Project Management Institute (PMI), the leading authority in project management, stated that 72% of projects failed that started and ended in 2008 (PMI, 2009). IT projects made up 86% of an organization project portfolio (University of Bremen, 2003). Information technology project management failures caused billions of dollars in damages for pharmaceutical companies and delayed drug product launch for millions of patients (PMI, 2009). In 2007, the Standish Group reported IT projects success rate were only at 35% (Cerpa & Verner, 2009). In 2011, project success was up slightly to 37% ("Failure rates finally drop," 2011). However, few qualitative studies contained detailed explanation of why these projects continue to fail. The research goal was not to confirm the other studies that projects did indeed fail, but aimed to understand why they failed.

In this study, the specific group was participants of pharmaceutical companies in Research Triangle Park, North Carolina. The qualitative research involved field study, which was appropriate for this study because the quest was for first-hand, lived experience of participants in their fields of work (Leedy & Ormrod, 2010). Also this study did not contain a quantification of data, but searched to understand the fundamental reasons behind IT projects failure in pharmaceutical companies (Neuman, 2006). The researcher wanted actively to participate in this study, and researcher's hands-on participation was the foundation of qualitative research (Willis, 2007). Chapter one contained the following parts that included (a) background, (b) problem statement, (c) purpose of the study, (d) significance of this study, (e) nature of this study, (f) research questions, (g) framework, (h) definitions, (i) assumptions, (j) scope with limitations/delimitations, and (k) the summary.

Background

The contribution of IT projects to drug development was significant. IT projects had been an enabler of drug development productivity improvement (Bardhan, Krishnan, & Lin, 2007). Information technology (IT) directly linked to every stage of the drug life cycle: drug discovery, drug development, and manufacturing of the drugs (Woo, Wolfgang, & Batista, 2008). The first stage of drug development was to discover new compounds that have potential to control a specific disease (Sekhon & Kamboj, 2010). From discovery of the compound to full drug approval by the US Food and Drug Administration (FDA) demanded on average of 10 years (Bhogal & Balls, 2008). During those 10 years, 92% of drugs in development never made it to market (Tobbell, 2009). Even without delay, a single drug required an average of 12 years and $1.3 Billion to take a drug to market ("Project zero," 2009). Some drugs can take up to 15 years and billions of dollars in investment according to the Pharmaceutical Research and Manufacturers of America (Jacquot, 2009). During those 10 years, the average financial cost of drug research and development was over $800 million, and one recent drug approval required $1.8 billion in research and development funding (Bharath et al., 2011). Only 8% of drug development programs made it to the FDA approval stage, and FDA offered no guarantees it will approve the submissions (Bhogal & Balls, 2008). However, using computer aided drug design (CADD), researchers used IT to select highly dependable compounds thus may prevent failures later in the drug approval process (Bharath, et al., 2011). Microfluidic technology was a key technology for drug discovery because it was a better technology for producing chemical articles and rapidly screening them against biological components (Sekhon & Kamboj, 2010). Microfluidic technology permitted multiple experiments running in parallel on small media device (Sekhon & Kamboj, 2010).

In the drug development phase, implementations of a number of technology programs accelerated drug development over the years by using software to automate mathematical models that previously scientists completed manually (Kaitin, 2010). Another example of IT speeding up drug discovery was the use of systems biology databases (Bhogal & Balls, 2008). A central database contained biological data from many sources which enabled research sharing of information. Knowledge workers used data mining technology to rapidly categorize human biological systems down to the molecular components level (Varu & Khanna, 2010). Microfluidics technology permitted quick screening of more drugs in shorter amount of time, which would cut down costs of developing drugs (Sekhon & Kamboj, 2010). During screening, computer aided drug designer (CADD) can further add value by predicting safety of the new drugs by analyzing toxic endpoints (Bharath, et al., 2011). Table 1 below showed drug development designation areas, and information technology programs that enabled the capabilities of each area. Each major drug development process required an enabling technology to expedite further development (Bhogal & Balls, 2008).

Table 1

Drug Development Designation and Enabling Technologies

Designation Process	**Enabling Information Technologies**
Genomics	DNA sequencing
Functional genomics	mRNA transcription profiling
Proteomics	Spectrometry, Electrophoresis, and antibody array
Metabolomics/ Metabanomics	Chromatography and mass spectrometry
Cytomics Cellomics	Digital imaging
Hyperquantitative tissue analysis	High resolution digital imaging
Clinical informatics	Informatical databases along with algorithms and data mining

Note. Adapted from Bhogal and Balls (2008).

In drug manufacturing, Americans had the world's safest drug supplies and the best consumer protection because IT played a vital part of ensuring this outcome (Wurst & Guernsey, 2006). For example, radiofrequency identification (RFID) can locate and authenticate critical drugs during the shipment process (Woo, et al., 2008). IT aided in verification of certified manufacturers and importers of raw materials by linking up with FDA databases that followed drug making best practices (Woo, et al., 2008). The use of enterprise resource planning (ERP) technology permitted manufacturing with fewer defects, higher quality, and increased predictability (Varu & Khanna, 2010). IT systems organized data to be readily available for inspection and audit (Varu & Khanna, 2010).

In short, clearly there was a direct correlation between the drug development life cycle and IT. For development of drugs to be successful, IT projects needed to be successful, as well. At time of this writing, there was no literature review that showed consistent, successful IT project management.

Problem Statement

The general problem addressed in this current study was the analysis and explanation of the high failure rate of IT projects in pharmaceutical industry. The failure rate of IT projects was greater than 72% (PMI, 2009). In 2007, the Standish Group reported IT projects success rate were only at 35% (Cerpa & Verner, 2009). In 2011, project success was up slightly to 37% ("Failure rates finally drop," 2011). The high failure rate delayed drug development. People were dependent on drugs to cure troublesome diseases and other ailments. Some people even depended on drugs to save their lives or the lives of loved ones. Drug development was not fast enough for some patients because many factors led to delays in launching new drug products (Kaitin, 2010). A delay in drug launch set back a company on average $15 million per day on each drug (Noffke, 2007). Drug launch delay (a) diminished a company to earn back research and development cost, (b) left door open for competition to release their versions of similar drugs, and (c) left patients waiting for a safe treatment option (Noffke, 2007). One critical factor leading to drug delay was the IT projects that supported drug development were constantly taking longer than expected (Civan & Maloney, 2009).

The specific problem was the lack of comprehension about the reasons that IT projects failed at such a high rate. A report by PMI stated poor project management and implementation skills were two key factors in project failures (PMI, 2009). Failures in information technology projects delayed the delivery of drugs to patients which needed the drugs to get better and live longer (PMI, 2009). The problem was that information technology projects in pharmaceutical companies continue to fail because of (a) finishing late, (b) over-budget, or with (c) low quality causing delays in drug development to save people's lives. For example, Pfizer Pharmaceutical's Lipitor cholesterol drug delay would cost the company $35 million per day (Noffke, 2007). The latest report showed 42 million Americans suffered from high cholesterol, and this drug delay would limit their treatment options (WebMD, 2012). Drug development cost on only one drug could be as high as $2 billion, so drug companies were eager to recoup drug cost quickly (Mikhail & Giddings, 2011).

The current study represented a phenomenological research design within a qualitative research method. As the objective of this current study was to analyze the IT projects failures phenomenon through the first-hand experiences of project team members and stakeholders who participated with the projects, a phenomenological research design was suitable for the current qualitative study. Qualitative research was appropriate over quantitative for this study because the focus was to answer "why" projects were continuing to fail at a high rate (Leedy & Ormrod, 2010). IT projects were unique, had clear starts and end dates, and added functionalities to hardware, software, or network infrastructure components (PMI, 2008). People planned, implemented, and controlled IT projects with focus on formal project management methodology (PMI, 2008). The general population of the current study was the project managers, team members, and stakeholders in the Research Triangle Park, North Carolina pharmaceutical companies. The stakeholders were in positions of authorities in dealing with the project management activities of the IT projects, such as Director of Projects, Director of ERP, and Vice President (VP) of IT.

Purpose of Study

The purpose of this qualitative phenomenological study was to explore the perceptions of 15 IT personnel from pharmaceutical companies in Research Triangle Park in Raleigh, North Carolina who witnessed first-hand on what factors caused project failures. Phenomenological research was a popular qualitative research strategy for the last 20 years (Shank, 2006). Phenomenological research was about the assumption that subjects of research have a conscious and can communicate with the researcher (Willis, 2007). Phenomenological research distinguished between noumena or real things and the perceptions of them or phenomena (Willis, 2007, p. 172). Therefore, phenomenological research focused on consciousness and perceptions (Neuman, 2006). The main task of phenomenological research was identifying common themes in people's descriptions of their own perceptions on how the projects failed (Leedy & Ormrod, 2010). Researchers obtained data for phenomenological research by interviewing and questioning participants (Willis, 2007). A researcher's goal was to understand a participant's experience and perceptions of the situation (Leedy & Ormrod, 2010).

The goal of the study was to provide descriptions of the key points on why projects failed. Qualitative research method permitted a focal point on understanding the problem in details based on experiences and first-hand eyewitness account, qualitative research method was most appropriate for this study (Neuman, 2006). The use of interview questioning approach helped in probing detailed description of the participants' first-hand accounts (Ojiako, Johansen, & David, 2008).

The phenomenological approach was the correct choice for this study. Phenomenological study used purposive sampling to select a specific population from the general population of project team members, stakeholders, and project managers (Leedy & Ormrod, 2010). The location for this study was Research Triangle Park, North Carolina, home to several major pharmaceutical companies.

Significance of the Study

Qualitative research was a technique to understand human and social behaviors (Willis, 2007). Qualitative research was the result of over a hundred years of development (Shank, 2006). The two main characteristics of qualitative research were (a) to search for contextual understanding and (b) to help distinguish an interpretation of an experience (Neuman, 2006).

With drug development exclusive dependency on IT projects, the faith of human lives relied on the success of these IT projects. IT projects involved intense human behaviors and interactions because people from different cultures, speaking different languages, and exercising different leadership styles made up a project team. The researcher tried to advance the literature by analyzing past failures in IT project management. The ultimate goal was to explore strategies that can lead to effective project management.

Significance of the Study to Leadership

The outcomes of this phenomenological study may assist scholar-practitioners leaders to better understand why IT projects failed and gained skills to change outcomes of projects implementation to be more successful. Scholars can use the findings and to integrate academic knowledge related to IT project management in pharmaceutical companies. Leadership practitioners could learn from the findings to achieve more success for IT projects.

Good leadership in project management can lead to improvement in quality of deliverables and boost in morale (Martin, Pearson, & Furumo, 2007). Companies' executives saw delivering projects as a key value driver to meet strategic objectives (Martin, Perrson, & Furumo, 2007). Developing proper project management leadership can lead an organization to improve reputation, reduce cost, reduce re-work, and to take on larger projects to align with strategic missions (Hurt & Thomas, 2009).

Nature of the Study

The causes of IT projects failures in pharmaceutical companies were not thoroughly understood. The current study included an effort to understand the first-hand experiences of project team members and stakeholders involved in the IT projects. To achieve this understanding, qualitative phenomenological was the best method (Leedy & Ormrod, 2010).

Research Method

This researcher considered quantitative, qualitative, and mixed method options for this study. Qualitative researchers aimed to (a) understand particular phenomenon, (b) develop new perspectives about the phenomenon, and/or (c) discover the problems of the phenomenon (Leedy & Ormrod, 2010). Willis (2007) stated, "It is not a method or research technique that determines whether something is qualitative research; it is how the study is conceived, what is to be accomplished, and how the data are understood" (p. 150).

In phenomenological research, the collection of extensive data on the participants' project management experience, training, and opinions were necessary. The use of data analysis spiral aided in categorizing data into the different phases of a project from requirements, code, testing, and project closure to identify any themes (Leedy & Ormrod, 2010). Other methods of data collection included observations, interviews, and any written documents, such as a project plan or project charter because these were effective for a qualitative research (Aramo-Immonen & Vanharanta, 2009). This researcher provided privacy and ethics expectations to potential candidates, so they were fully aware of the procedure of the study (Neuman, 2006). The incentive for the participants was to discover what and how other organizations were more successful in IT project management. Maybe the participants can implement the strategies that proven to be successful within their organizations.

Research Design

As the main purpose of the study was to explore the first-hand experience of participants, phenomenological research study included analysis of the central phenomenon of why IT projects failed at a high rate. The phenomenological research design was appropriate for this study because interviewing the participants to understand the central phenomenon to reach awareness (Neuman, 2006). During analysis of data, one can categorize the answers into various perceptions of the phenomenon meanings (Leedy & Ormrod, 2010).

Triangulation of Results

Triangulation assured validity of the research by overcoming limitations and bias (Willis, 2007). A key type of triangulation was data triangulation involving time, space, and people (Leedy & Ormrod, 2010). This study contained analysis of data collected from interviewing diverse people, on different days, and at dissimilar locations.

Research Questions/Hypotheses

By studying project management best practices, the research questions guided the researcher through an interview process with participants and enabled detection of common themes phenomenon (Leedy & Ormrod, 2010). Project Management Institute (PMI) was the leading authority on project management, and this researcher referenced PMI best practices books in this study (PMI, 2008).

RQ1: What factors cause information technology projects to continue failing at a high rate?

RQ2: What effect does project management software such as Microsoft Project have on project failures?

RQ3: What leadership characteristics do successful project managers have?

RQ4: What effect does PMI training and certification of project managers have on failure experiences?

Conceptual or Theoretical Framework

Phenomenological researchers sought unbiased treatment of the research subjects, so they should block any preconceived theories or personal experience for better focus on what the participants were stating (Leedy & Ormrod, 2010). Interpretative phenomenological analysis (IPA) can give a detailed picture based on what the participants explained from their experiences (Pringle, Drummond, McLafferty, & Hendry, 2011). In phenomenological research, each participant had a different experience, and one must analyze and triangulate to find a phenomenon.

Broad Theoretical Area of This Study

The broad theoretical area of this study was under IT project management in pharmaceutical industry. This study included an analysis on the use of project management best practices and projects success rates. Numerous research and descriptions of best practices in project management existed, yet projects continued to fail (Edington & Ouellette, 2011). Studies showed that the lack of implementation of project management best practices was a leading reason for project failure (Besner, & Hobbs, 2008). Several other reports concluded lack of proper project risk management was a main reason for failures (Benţa, Podean, & Mircean, 2011).

The use of project management best practices may add structure to an organization attempts to deliver a project on time, within budget, and with quality (Edington & Ouellette, 2011). Project monitoring and reporting were critical to project governance and evaluation of project progress (Besner, & Hobbs, 2008). This study included an analysis if project management best practices adoption throughout the each organization's project life-cycle. Additional analysis included understanding if best practices used in daily, occasionally, or only when a project deadline was in jeopardy.

This study included analysis of leadership theories' effects on project success. A strong correlation existed between project success and good leadership (Ong, Richardson, Yanqing, Qile, & Johnson, 2009). Despite introduction of new technology and tools to aid in project management, a project success was largely dependent on leadership (Gudarzi & Chegin, 2011). Management of people required more than the use of common project management tools and techniques (Ong et al., 2009).

As for the leadership side of project management, effective leadership can aid in development of a culture of learning and trust (Ong et al., 2009). Project managers who had reputations for stronger leadership skills than their peers usually were more successful project managers (Gudarzi & Chegin, 2011). Effective leadership promoted integration of efforts across functional groups (Lloyd-Walker & Walker, 2011).

Project leadership enabled change management because change cannot happen unless someone led the initiative for change (Lloyd-Walker & Walker, 2011). Providing leadership needed to make changes was critical because some organizations were resistant to change (Gudarzi & Chegin, 2011). A project was about making changes to a process, product, or service (Ong et al., 2009).

Important Issues, Perspectives, and Controversies in IT Project Management in Pharmaceutical Industry

Important Issues

The issue was failure of IT projects lead to drug delays that could cost companies billions of dollars, and people can lose loved ones and friends because the drug they depended on was not ready (Tobbell, 2009). The trend showed that IT projects continued to fail year over year, so a better understanding was necessary (Cerpa & Verner, 2009). Literally, lives were at stake.

Perspectives

The perception was pharmaceutical executives did not know how to sponsor or led IT projects to success (Jani, 2011). Different studies showed data stating that projects failed, and some explained why (Keil & Mähring, 2010). However, the results of these studies were from most industries, and not focusing only on pharmaceutical industry (Kaitin, 2010).

Controversies

Controversies involved disagreements between what leadership theories were best for project management (Lloyd-Walker & Walker, 2011). Other controversies included the complexity of IT projects because of evolving technology and what tools were appropriate to manage the project's day to day activities (Benţa, Podean, & Mircean, 2011). Furthermore, controversies existed between project stakeholders, project managers, and other project team members on how to navigate through the project life cycle (Damaré, 2008).

Historical, Germinal, and Current literature in IT Project Management in Pharmaceutical Industry

Historical

Modern day project management began with the Manhattan Project, which was the project that led to development of the first nuclear bomb in the 1940s (Lenfle & Loch, 2010). The result of formal project management was the creation of the first ever atomic bomb that led to an ally victory and an end to World War II (Lenfle & Loch, 2010). In the early 1960s, Secretary of Defense, Robert McNamara, introduced project evaluation review technique (PERT) and phased approach to the project management standard (Lenfle & Loch, 2010). Between 1987 and 1996, project management articles began to heavily favor IT project management (Rivard & Dupré, 2009).

Along with formal project management, today's formal pharmaceutical drug development management started in the 1940s. The interconnected relationships between drug companies, academic researchers, and medical doctors which led to today's pharmaceutical industry started in the 1940s, as well (Tobbell, 2009). Strengthening pharmaceutical knowledge continued in the post- World War II years, and drug scientists researched and collaborated with academic researchers and medical professionals to develop drugs (Tobbell, 2009). To accelerate drug development and gain FDA approval faster, pharmaceutical companies relied on information technology to help in achieving this goal. The global pharmaceutical industry was more dependent on information technology than any other sector (Athreye & Godley, 2009).

Germinal

The Project Management Institute (PMI) formed in the late 1960s, and continued to be a critical training and development center for IT project managers (Rivard & Dupré, 2009). PMI was a globally recognized standard and authority of IT project management (Rivard & Dupré, 2009). PMI conducted a survey of its members and found that 28% of IT projects did not finish on time or within budget (PMI, 2009).

Current Literature

Keil and Mähring (2010) collected data on hundreds of IT projects over 17 years and reviewed that many reasons can cause a project to fail. Cerpa and Verner (2009) researched 70 failed IT projects and stated that billions of dollars wasted each year because of failed IT projects. Although many articles and journals contained information on IT projects failures, few provided failure information specific to the pharmaceutical industry.

Fit of Study within IT Project Management in Pharmaceutical Industry

People depended on drugs to cure ailments and to live healthier and longer. Pharmaceutical companies depended on drug development and information technology projects, which were critical to drug development success. Findings from the literature review supported the fit of this study for IT project management in pharmaceutical industry.

Definitions

This study used key terms to establish common definition of the research. The terms below were used throughout the study: (a) project failure, (b) IT projects, (c) project manager, (d) project team members, (e) stakeholders, (f) software development life cycle (SDLC), and (g) project management.

Here were definitions of the key terms:

Project failure: a project failed to finish on time, within budget, or/and with quality (PMI, 2009).

IT projects: a project that included creating or enhancing functionality to hardware, software, or/and network infrastructure (Karlsen et al., 2005).

Project manager: the person accountable for the project assigned, also known as the leader of the individual project (Lenfle & Loch, 2010).

Project team members: people assigned to the project to complete tasks within the project (Nwachukwu, 2010).

Stakeholders: Usually stakeholders were high ranking executives within the organization with budget authority. The project manager reported to one or more stakeholders (Ojiako et al, 2008).

Software development life cycle: The phases that made up a project's progress from beginning to end (Sridhar, 2010).

Project management: The methodology used to start, implement, and close-out a project (Armon-Immonen & Vanharanta, 2009).

Scope, Limitations, and Delimitations, Transferability of Results

The scope of the study included stakeholders, project managers, and project team members who had first-hand experiences of failed IT projects and had an understanding of what reasons led to those failures. These participants offered their lived experiences to this phenomenological study. As a reminder, a project was a failure when it did not finish on time, within budget, and with quality (PMI, 2009). These participants should be able to take the researcher through the software development life cycle phases of the IT projects.

Limitations

Limitations were challenges or flaws to the study (Neuman, 2006). This study contained limitations combined with (a) location of participants, (b) participant cooperation level, and (c) over-generalization. The participants in this research study were from the geography of Research Triangle Park, North Carolina. The limiting factor was the study's data was representation of Research Triangle Park only and did not include reasoning why IT projects failed in other geographies.

Another limitation was the small participant sample size of 15 to explore why IT projects failed. The participants were selected from surveys collected at the local PMI chapter in Research Triangle Park. The answers in the surveys identified the industries they worked in, level of experience in project management, and roles in the projects. The participants were stakeholders, project managers, and project team members who participated with IT projects in the pharmaceutical industry. The stakeholders provided details on when and why they thought the projects started failing. The project managers offered details on the initial categories of the project management process. Project team members provided yet another level of details because they were intimate to certain phases of the project management process. Combined, these participants produced insight to the IT projects failure phenomenon. The findings were from Research Triangle Park IT projects, but may lead to over-generalization that IT projects outside of the geographic area may have the same findings. To address the overgeneralization potential, the study included specific factors from the details of the interviews on the phenomenon of why IT projects failed in the pharmaceutical industry (Neuman, 2006).

Purposeful sampling for this study was a limitation because the researcher picked participants that were fit-for-purpose based on the categories in this study and did not use random sampling. Researcher created a purposive sampling, which could lead to bias when compared to pure random selection (Leedy & Ormrod, 2010). Purpose sampling was necessary to seek out participants on projects in pharmaceutical companies only. These participants were stakeholders, project managers, or project team members. The limitation was purposeful sampling may not be as convincing as a completely random sampling study, which would be more exhaustive.

Delimitation

Delimitations were the limits on a study based on what the researcher planed to cover or not cover (Willis, 2007). A delimitation of the current study was the target population of stakeholders, project managers, and project team members within 30 minutes driving distance of the researcher. The participants explained that they had lived experiences of failed IT projects. This researcher selected only participants from pharmaceutical companies in Research Triangle Park, North Carolina.

Transferability of Results

Qualitative researchers aimed for generalizability, so other researchers must decide on application of transferability of the results by considering the details (Leedy & Ormrod, 2010). This researcher provided details on the backgrounds of participants, locations of study, and roles on the projects. Research method and design were available in the appropriate sections in the following chapters.

Assumptions

One assumption of this study was the belief that stakeholders, project managers, and team members shared similar views on each project's performance. Second, the participants of the study added value to the research by providing meaningful information. Third, the participants were honest and their memories clear. Another assumption was a true and honest discussion as the participants did not hold back on their contributions to the IT project failures. Because this study was a phenomenological study, which meant use of a small sample size, so this researcher placed a heavy emphasis on the quality of information (Pringle et al., 2011). The final assumption was that each project followed a methodology or project management process similar to the software development life cycle (SDLC).

Summary

Chapter 1 contained introduction to the topic of how information technology project management failures caused billions of dollars in damages for pharmaceutical companies and delayed drug product launch for millions of patients (PMI, 2009). Managing a project was a complex process (Wurst & Guernsey, 2006). According to Project Management Institute (PMI), only 28% of information technology projects finished on time, within budget, and with quality (2009). Every project was dependent on an information technology component (PMI, 2008). The purpose of this study was to analyze why IT projects in the pharmaceutical industry continued to fail, so company executives can take corrective actions to enhance success potential.

To understand the failure phenomenon of IT projects in pharmaceutical companies, the current qualitative phenomenological study included a detailed analysis of the experiences from 15 stakeholders, project managers, and project team members who were intimately involved with IT projects tasks in Research Triangle Park, North Carolina. The outcomes of this study may help to increase the success rates of future IT projects in pharmaceutical industry. Literally, lives were at stake, so this study was imperative to people's livelihood and their families. Chapter 2 covered the review of literature on project management and pharmaceutical industry with focus on drug development. Researcher also examined leadership theories and project management phases. The diversity of research material was highlighted in Chapter 2.

Chapter 2: Review of the Literature

The purpose of this qualitative phenomenological study was to study the first-hand experiences of 15 stakeholders, project managers, and team members in IT projects of pharmaceutical companies in Research Triangle Park, North Carolina. The purpose of this literature review was to provide historical perspectives on information technology (IT) project management and pharmaceutical organizations' dependency on IT for drug development. The literature review contained assessment of project management best practices from Project Management Institute (PMI) and Agile Project Management. The literature review confirmed the value of this study because further potential development in pharmaceutical project management. The literature review highlighted the importance of IT projects on drug research, yet projects' effective rates continued to be low. Completing a formal literature review can lead to an "unbiased, complete, and reproducible" study (Boell & Cecez-Kecmanovic, 2010, p. 130).

The main objective of chapter 2 was to review the historical and current literature between years 2007 and 2012 on IT projects that failed in pharmaceutical companies. The results of this literature review substantiated the gaps in literature today of how IT projects can be more successful in pharmaceutical companies. By researching journals, articles, and books to shape the foundation of the research topics, this chapter 2 included historical overviews and general methodologies of project management and drug development. Given the vast availability of information on both topics, this review was not an exhaustive or complete evaluation; rather the review contained general experiences of resources on failed IT projects in pharmaceutical industry.

Title Searches, Articles, and Journals

The literature review included key word searches on more than 400 peer-reviewed articles, journals, and other studies mostly from 2007 to 2012 or within five years. Searches consisted of an assortment of similar topics adjoining on project management, project failure, IT projects, project manager, project team members, stakeholder governance, software development life cycle (SDLC), agile project methodology, and project management. Key word searches included "projects success," "project failures," "leadership theories," "leadership and project management," "project management," "project management best practices," "information technology projects," "information technology and drug development," "cost of delays in drug development," "history of project management," and "history of drug development." Primary search source was the University of Phoenix – Library internet search tool, which included EBSCOhost, Gale PowerSearch, ProQuest, Books 24x7, ITECH netBASE, Oxford Scholarship Online, and Library Information Science & Technology Abstracts (LISTA) databases. Researcher only referenced relevant and related information to aid in answering the research questions of IT project management and pharmaceutical drug development for this literature review. Of the 400 peer-reviewed articles, journals, and other studies reviewed, 88 referenced in this study. The peer-reviewed articles and journals were mostly from publishing organizations catering to professionals in project management and drug development. Books were from leaders in organizational theories and leadership philosophies.

The Literature

This literature review summarized the history IT project management evolution as well as the role of IT in pharmaceutical drug development. The literature review substantiated the need to continue this research because the importance of drug development and the lack of effectiveness in IT project management specific to the pharmaceutical industry. Information in this review may establish the need for awareness of the importance of IT projects in pharmaceutical companies because the delays caused billions of dollars in damages and keep millions of patients waiting for life saving drugs (PMI, 2009).

Throughout this literature review, researcher noticed two common themes. First, drug development had a higher dependency on IT systems than ever before to launch drugs to market (Bharath, Manjula, & Vijaychand, 2011). Second, IT project failure cases far exceeded success stories (Karlsen, Anderen, Birkely, & Odega, 2005). Keil and Mähring (2010) collected data on hundreds of IT projects over 17 years and reviewed that many reasons can cause a project to fail. Cerpa and Verner (2009) researched 70 failed IT projects and stated that IT knowledge workers wasted billions of dollars in pay and other costs each year because of failed IT projects. Although many articles and journals contained information on IT projects failures, few provided failure information specific to the pharmaceutical industry. The literature suggested many types of IT projects usually failed at critical phases of the project life cycle (Lenfle & Loch, 2010). The literature review confirmed the supposition that a need to understand the phenomena of why IT projects failed in pharmaceutical companies. This understanding could raise the leadership awareness to identify and turn around troubled projects before they became another case study of project failures.

Framework of Research Literature

An examination into areas around the phenomena under investigation in this study was to uncover themes to establish relationships between sources and an explanation of types of literature researched and referenced in this study (see Figures 1 and 2 below). This literature review demonstrated comprehensiveness in breadth, relevance, availability, and depth of topics and raised awareness to gaps that could be addressed in future studies.

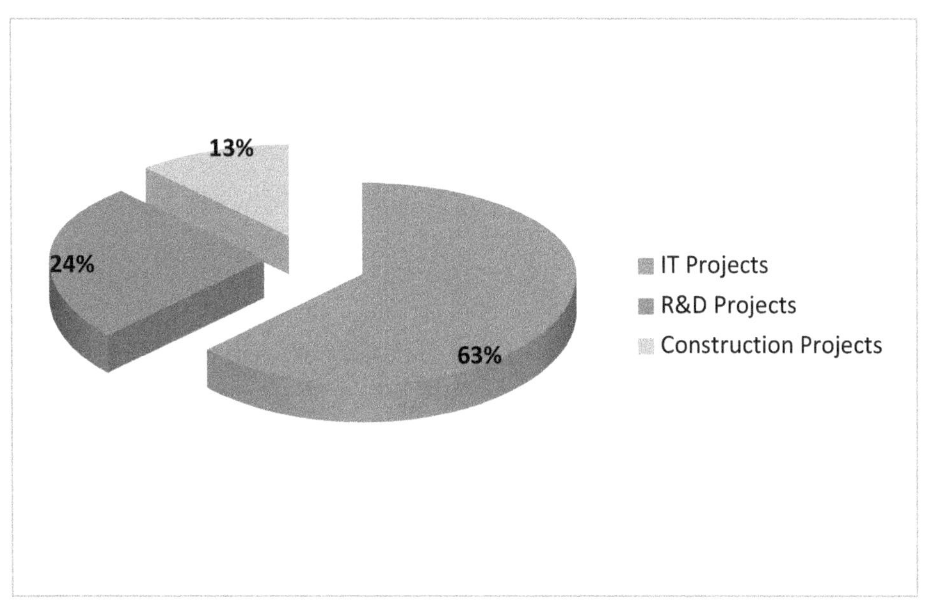

Figure 1: Percentage of Articles on Types of Projects (PMI, 2009)

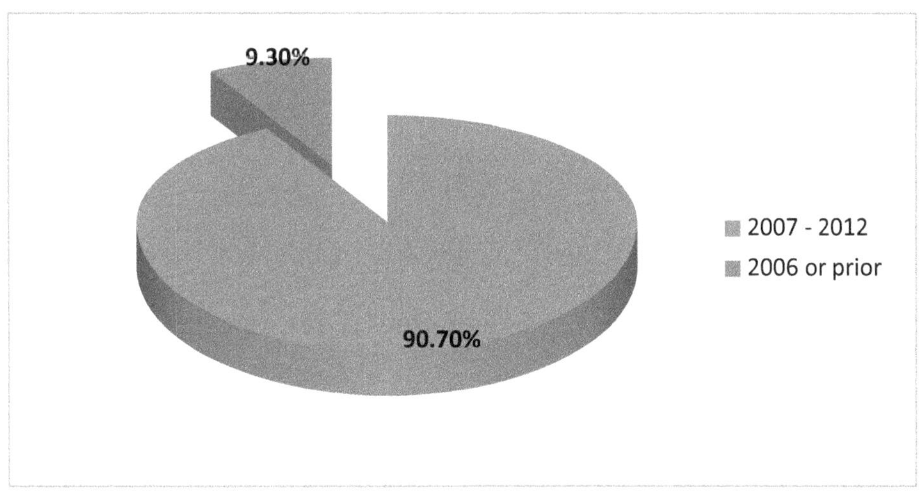

Figure 2: Literature Maturity

Theoretical Bases of IT Project Management

Stakeholders, project managers, and project team members adapted several leadership models and theories in their dealings with project management activities. The three primary goals of any project were to finish (a) on time, (b) on budget, and (c) with quality (PMI, 2008). To reach these goals, project leaders often drew from different theories and models to solve problems that they encountered throughout the project phases (Oswick, Fleming, & Hanlon, 2011). IT project leaders used the following models and theories to develop software and other information systems (a) Frederick Taylor's scientific management theory, (b) Vroom-Yetton Jago Decision Model, (c) Rogers' diffusion of innovation theory, (d) Henri Fayol's management theory, and (e) Douglas McGregor's Theory X and Y (Weiyin, Thong, Chasalow, & Dhillon, 2011).

Frederick Taylor's Scientific Management Theory

Frederick Taylor was the father of scientific management (Blake & Moseley, 2011). Scientific management involved having a leader for the work tasks, developing a plan, and teamwork was essential in completing these tasks (Myers Jr., 2011). Also a worker would perform a job function that he or she had knowledge of (Brogan, 2011). One of Taylor's students was Henry Gantt, and Henry developed the Gantt chart, which was a commonly used project management tool for IT projects (Darmody, 2007). The point here was scientific management may be the foundation of today's project management (Darmody, 2007).

Vroom Yetton Jago Decision Model

Project leaders must make decisions to manage the project successfully. Because IT projects were different in design, the leadership style needed to adapt to the project situation (Stancu & Rece, 2010). Vroom Yetton Jago decision model involved a tree-like decision making structure to guide a leader on choosing one of five different leadership styles of (a) autocratic type 1, (b) autocratic type 2, (c) consultative type 1, (d) consultative type 2, and (e) group-based type 2 with details listed below (De Meuse, Dai, & Hallenbeck, 2010).

Autocratic Type 1: Project leader made own decision and did not consult the project team.

Autocratic Type 2: Project leader sought information from project team members, but made decisions alone.

Consultative Type 1: Project leader consulted project team members individually on an as-needed basis, but ultimately made decision alone.

Consultative Type 2: Project leader consulted project teams and encouraged team collaboration on alternative solutions, but ultimately made decision alone.

Group-based Type 2: Project leader sought team consensus and decision approved by team.

Everett Rogers' Diffusion of Innovation Theory

Everett Rodgers explained diffusion of innovation theory as how society adapted innovation (Soffer, Nachmias, & Ram, 2010). In this study's context, an innovation was a new technology or service that required a project to implement the innovation. Three fundamentals of diffusion of innovation theory were (a) how innovation spread, (b) significance of social networking, and (c) different needs by different customers (Lovejoy, Demireva, Grayson, & McNamara, 2009). As for adaptation of innovation, Rodgers stated five aspects below that determined how quickly society accepts innovation (Soffer, Nachmias, & Ram, 2010).

Relative advantage: What made this new product, service, or idea better than an alternate opportunity?

Compatibility with existing values and practices: The new innovation needed to be consistent with existing ethical and other standards.

Simplicity and ease of use: Learning this new innovation should be easy. The more difficult to pick up, the more difficult it was for the innovation to spread.

Trialability: Researchers tested the new innovation in selected market to target audience before expansion.

Observable results: The innovation must show improvements once an adopter used the new produce, service, or idea.

Henri Fayol's Management Theory

One research question focused on leadership style and project management success. Henri Fayol's Management Theory had key objectives that mirrored the project management life cycle theory (Pryor & Taneja, 2010). Henri Fayol was known as the father of modern operational management theory (Pryor & Taneja, 2010). Fayol's theory contrasted from Frederick Taylor's theory because Fayol looked at management from the executive view, but Taylor focused on the individual worker skill levels (McLean, 2011). However, this current study can benefit from having a top-down and bottom-up analysis of pharmaceutical project management. Fayol identified five primary objectives for management as (a) planning, (b) managing, (c) commanding, (d) facilitating, and (e) controlling (McLean, 2011). To supplement these objectives, Fayol also explained the 14 principles of management listed below (Pryor & Taneja, 2010):

1. Specialization of labor: project team members continued to improve their skills.

2. Authority: project managers had the right to command.
3. Discipline: project leader can discipline when orders were not followed.
4. Unity of command: Each project had one project manager/leader.
5. Unity of direction: Each project followed one project plan.
6. Subordination of individual interests: Project team members primarily discussed project activities not personal agendas
7. Remuneration: Stakeholders, project managers, and project team members were financially compensated fairly.
8. Centralization: Executives provided the leadership and direction for the team.
9. Chain of Superiors: Each employee had a supervisor.
10. Order: Employees had a place for work such as offices or cubicles assigned to them.
11. Equity: Employees expected and received fair treatment (no harassment).
12. Personnel Tenure: Management should try to keep good employees happy, so they stayed longer with the company.
13. Initiative: Planned and implemented (do not just talk about; do it).
14. Esprit de corps: Management should strive for harmony on project teams.

Douglas McGregor's Theory X and Y

Douglas McGregor proposed two theories in explaining employees' motivation: Theory X and Theory Y. Management should use Theory X and Y to make decisions in the best interest of production levels at their companies (Kopelman, Prottas, & Davis, 2008). Theory X characterized a typical employee seeks to avoid work, followed rather than led, did not care about company's goals, did not like change, was not very smart (Cunningham, 2011). As for Theory Y, McGregor assumed an average employee enjoyed work, committed to work objectives, expected rewards for meeting work objectives, wanted increasing responsibility, and took on more responsibilities (Kopelman, Prottas, & Davis, 2008).

Historical Review of IT Project Management

As mentioned earlier, modern day project management began with the Manhattan Project, which led to the development of the first nuclear bomb in the 1940s (Lenfle & Loch, 2010). Project management processes continued to evolve during the development of the ballistic missile projects, Atlas and Polaris, of the 1950s (Lenfle & Loch, 2010). These two projects contained examples of organization, planning, and discipline that were the cores of standard IT project management. The result of formal project management was the creation of the first ever atomic bomb that led to an ally victory and end to World War II (Lenfle & Loch, 2010). For the Atlas and Polaris missile projects, leaders introduced project management framework of steering committee, dedicated team, and development of a project plan (Lenfle & Loch, 2010). In the early 1960s, Secretary of Defense, Robert McNamara introduced project evaluation review technique (PERT) and phased approach to the project management standard (Lenfle & Loch, 2010). The Project Management Institute (PMI) formed in the late 1960s, and continued to be a critical training and development center for IT project managers (Rivard & Dupré, 2009). Between 1987 and 1996, project management articles heavily favored IT project management (Rivard & Dupré, 2009). PMI was a globally recognized standard and authority of IT project management (Rivard & Dupré, 2009). PMI conducted a survey of its members and found that 28% of IT projects did not finish on time or within budget (PMI, 2009).

Historical Review of Pharmaceutical Industry

Project management was not the only discipline that started seriously in the 1940s. The intertwining relationships between drug companies, academic researchers, and medical doctors who led to today's pharmaceutical industry best practices started in the 1940s, as well (Tobbell, 2009). The strengthening of pharmaceutical knowledge continued in the postwar years, and drug scientists researched and collaborated with academic researchers and medical professionals to develop drugs (Tobbell, 2009). Fruition of new drugs such, as antibiotics, cortisone, and tranquilizers in the 1940s was the results of this new research-based drug development strategy (Tobbell, 2009). In the 1960s, government regulations pushed for drug reforms that included the patent terms, which led to the rise of generics (Tobbell, 2009). Furthermore, drug amendments increased the authority of the Food and Drug Administration (FDA) that required strenuous testing before human consumptions (Tobbell, 2009).

To accelerate drug development and gain FDA approval faster, pharmaceutical companies relied on information technology to aid in achieving this goal. The global pharmaceutical industry was more dependent on information technology than any other sector (Athreye & Godley, 2009). The role of technology innovation was key in creating the emergence of new pharmaceutical leaders and destroyed those companies that did not embrace new technologies fast enough (Athreye & Godley, 2009). For example, Korean pharmaceutical companies leveraged information technology as a competitive advantage to distribute their drugs in new markets faster than other Asian companies (Athreye & Godley, 2009). US pharmaceutical firms became leaders in penicillin sales by using new information technology to manufacture the drugs more rapidly than the German pharmaceutical companies (Athreye & Godley, 2009).

Initial Categories of IT Projects

IT projects were projects that were unique, had clear starts and end dates, and added functionalities to hardware, software, or network infrastructure pieces (PMI, 2008). Knowledge workers planned, implemented, and controlled IT projects with focus on formal project management methodology (PMI, 2008). The top five most common IT projects across industries were feasibility studies, data migration projects, implementation projects, enhancement projects, and service management projects (Karlsen, et al., 2005). All five types of IT projects contained the same three success criterion of completing projects on (a) on time, (b) within cost, and (c) with quality (PMI, 2008).

Feasibility Studies

A feasibility or pilot study project was to determine a go/no-go decision for further funding and development of an IT idea (Arain, 2010). A feasibility study was a small-scale project that gave stakeholders impressions of the potential benefit of the full scale version (Arain, 2010). The results of a feasibility study can aid executives to decide if the organization had enough resources to pursue a new IT endeavor further (Arain, 2010). Feasibility studies were helpful in swiftly eliminating options considered too expensive or constraining for the company to pursue (Arain, 2010).

Implementation Projects

Implementation projects usually included development of a new IT application or service (Popa, 2010). A new internal web portal was as an example of an implementation project. Another example of an implementation project was development of a new mobile application to work with cellular phones.

Upgrade Projects

Similar to implementation projects were upgrade projects. However, these projects were to add functionality or fix bugs from a previous implementation projects (Olson & Zhao, 2007). For example, the company already had a web portal, but executives wanted to add functionality that permitted employees to check their 401K and salary information inside the web portal (Nah & Delgado, 2006). The addition was an upgrade to the existing web portal, so therefore it was an upgrade project.

Migration Projects

Migration projects were movement of IT hardware, software, or network infrastructure components to another location. For example, a company built a new data center and needed to move the IT components from old data center to new data center. The movement still required full life cycle processes of controlling and testing and was a migration project (Eckell, 2010).

Support Services Projects

Support services projects were development of new tools or services to aid in the support of IT infrastructure. For example, the setup of a call center to take calls from employees across the globe that had technical questions or issues when using the new web portal was a support services project (Pollard & Cater-Steel, 2009).

Project Management Methodology

Two main types of project management methodologies existed today for the development, implementation, and testing of IT projects. This information was important because these were the only two endorsed project management methodologies (PMI, 2009). The section below provided further context.

Waterfall / Software Development Life Cycle (SDLC)

The first and most used project management methodology was waterfall or software development life cycle (SDLC). The waterfall, like the name implied, divided an IT project down to sequential phases of requirements analysis, system design, coding, testing, deployment, and maintenance (Microsoft, 2006). Project Management Institute endorsed Waterfall/SDLC process (PMI, 2008).

Agile Development

Agile was an umbrella software development methodology that aimed to deliver production, higher quality, and increased effectiveness rate of software projects by focusing on delivered compartment size work package (Ionel, 2009). Unlike waterfall or SDLC, agile delivered a finished work package for each milestone. The relevance to one research question was to see if one type of project management methodology was more successful than the other.

Requirements Gathering Techniques

An important phase of project management, but usually neglected, was requirements gathering (Hands et al., 2004). Many people made assumptions on what the customers wanted, but did not really confirm. This phase started the stage for the whole project because most deliverables were requirements based.

Interview

Interview was the process of gathering requirements by asking the customers, users, and stakeholders exactly what they wanted to see in the finished product or service (Hands, et al., 2004). Communication was via verbal communication or hand-written with a focus on feedback of a prototype (Hands et al., 2004). By having detailed requirements, project leaders may face less re-work in project later.

JAD Session

Joint Application Development (JAD) was a requirements gathering process which a third party or independent person facilitates a meeting between customer/stake holders and project team members (Appan & Browne, 2010). The goal of JAD was to keep discussion unbiased because a project manager may steer the project toward the agenda. Also in JAD, a facilitator can keep the group focus on the requirements without going into different tangents of discussion.

Testing methodology

Testing was an important step in the project management life cycle. Usually success or failure can be predicted in the testing results. Also testing benefitted both software developers and customers by identifying errors before releasing product or service (Yang, et al., 2011).

Waterfall testing model

The waterfall testing was a phase in the software development life cycle (SDLC) in which testing came after product design (Microsoft, 2006). However, testing did not start until the completion of coding or programming phase. In agile testing, functional testing of the product was a key factor. Waterfall testing was in scope for this study because it was one of the most common types of testing in pharmaceutical IT projects (Woo, Woflgang, & Batista, 2008).

V Model

The V model testing was comprehensive testing where review, verification, and readiness are added to the testing process (Sridhar, 2010). The "V" name came from a top-down approach to requirements definition than a bottom-up to coding and development, which formed a V shape (Sridhar, 2010). The V model can aid in testing each phase of the software development life cycle (Liguo, 2008). This researcher excluded V model from this research because V models were too time consuming and complex for the typical pharmaceutical IT projects.

Spiral model

Spiral model was mainly about identifying risks in the product or service when testing on how the development can mitigate that risk (Boehm, 2007). For example, a risk was the security feature of new software, and the spiral testing would focus on hacking the software. Testers used spiral testing model to test programming prototypes (Qumer & Henderson-Sellers, 2008). Risk-based project management was in use frequently, so spiral testing was part of this study.

Agile testing model

Agile testing was a phase of agile project management where each work package was part of testing as it was delivered (Ionel, 2009). In waterfall project management, testing started when the project was finishing up instead when new functionality added. Agile permitted flexibility in changing business requirements (Nănău, 2010). Researcher included agile testing model in this study because it was very common in the pharmaceutical industry because of its marketing in saving testing time.

Reasons for IT Project Failures

Researchers collected data on hundreds of IT projects over 17 years and discovered that many reasons can cause a project to fail (Keil & Mähring, 2010). Simple reasons from not thinking that a project could fail to more difficult risks were uncovered during review (Jani, 2011). Another discovery was that most executives know that IT projects had high failure rates, and some large IT projects were black holes when significant human and financial resources were absorbed with no stoppage in sight (Keil & Mähring, 2010). For example, one IT project at the Federal Bureau of Investigation (FBI) already accumulated expenses of over $170 million, and the FBI Director had to end the project before it completed because no reliable cost ceiling could be projected (Keil & Mähring, 2010).

Cerpa and Verner (2009) researched 70 failed IT projects and stated that billions of dollars wasted each year because of failed IT projects. Furthermore, there was very little understanding of poor projects performance (Cerpa & Verner, 2009). Management also did not see preventing future failures as a priority, and little explanation uncovered why this trend continued (Cerpa & Verner, 2009). Initial findings of why projects failed included (a) aggressive delivery date, (b) poor project managers, (c) too many risks not accounted for, and (d) exhaustion from team members delayed the projects further (Cerpa & Verner, 2009).

Morris (2008) stated that up to 95 % of projects failed within the first five minutes because project managers were given a project with firm due date and fixed cost already attached. Projects did not fail without warnings; stakeholders stated they saw many red flags but did not act on them until it was too late (Wee-Kiat, Siew, & Adrian, 2011). The finding was just "as the reasons that a project fails had not changed, the objectives to keep a project from failing had not changed either" (Morris, 2008, p. 24).

Conclusion

One main conclusion derived from the literature review was that high failure rate of IT projects in pharmaceutical company was a major concern for executives, patients, and patients' loved ones (Al-Ahmad, Al-Fagih, Khanfar, Alsamara, Abuleil, & Abu-Salem, 2009). The literature review included an explanation on the value for this phenomenological study and highlighted the lack of knowledge in IT projects failures specific to pharmaceutical companies. Peer-reviewed journals and articles researched for this study provided information on IT projects failure rates, drug development dependency on IT projects, and researchers' assessment of why

IT projects failed. Researched showed many articles and journals existed highlighting IT projects failures in general, but few findings were specific to the pharmaceutical industry thus a gap existed.

This literature review contained information supporting the notion that IT projects continued to fail year over year with no reprisal identified (PMI, 2009; Cerpa & Verner, 2009). IT projects were vital to the development of drugs, and drugs were vital in saving people's lives (Bhogal & Balls, 2008). The review of the literature resulted in endorsement of the problem statement, purpose statement, and the research questions for this phenomenological study.

Summary

The main objective of chapter 2 was the review of the historical and current journals and articles between 2007 and 2012 on IT projects failures in pharmaceutical industry. The failures of IT projects led to delay in new drug launches (Kaitin, 2010). Because of the importance of drugs to sick people or the preventative nature of drugs, the reasons behind IT projects failures delaying drugs development needed to be understood (Sekhon & Kamboj, 2010).

Clearly, pharmaceutical companies were valuable to the human race because their employees made drugs that saved lives. The pharmaceutical companies depended heavily on information technology as a competitive advantage to deliver drugs of value more quickly than their competitors (Woo et al., 2008). Leaders in the pharmaceutical industry credited their use of information technology that led them to leapfrog the competition (Athreye & Godley, 2009). The literature review confirmed the need for this research since pharmaceutical company executives must figure out why their IT project success rates were not higher, so they can deliver drugs to save lives quicker. Further research was required to understand IT projects failures in pharmaceutical companies. Chapter 3 included a discussion on the research methodology for this phenomenological study.

Chapter 3: Study Context Methodology

The continued high failure rate of IT projects in pharmaceutical companies was the general problem that this study aimed to address. The specific problem was the lack of comprehension about the reasons why IT projects failed at such a high rate and what phases of a project did the failures occurred. Because of the importance of drugs to people with illnesses and prevention capabilities, the reasons behind IT projects failures delaying drugs development needed to be understood (Sekhon & Kamboj, 2010). Through the interviews of 15 stakeholders, project managers, and team members who had first-hand experiences of failed projects in pharmaceutical companies in Research Triangle Park, NC, this study examined the failure phenomenon.

Chapter 2 contained a literature review and gaps uncovered during review of IT projects failures in pharmaceutical companies. This study contained an investigation of what project types and phases did projects normally failed. Chapter 3 contained an explanation on the (a) research methodology and design appropriateness, (b) sampling size, (c) selection process of the participants, (d) confidentiality, (e) informed consent, (f) data collection, (g) instrumentation, (h) internal and external validity, (i) reliability and (j) the data analysis from interviews.

Research Method and Design

Rationale for Appropriateness of the Research Method & Design

Qualitative research method offered many advantages over quantitative research for this study. Researchers used qualitative research to aid in understanding a new phenomenon (Sandbaek, 2006). Qualitative researchers looked into understanding the big picture of the topic of study (Sandbaek, 2006). Qualitative researchers used inductive reasoning thinking where theories moved from specific to general or also known as a bottom-up approach (Elo & Kyngas,

2008). A key disadvantage of qualitative research was biased in design of study and data collection process (Elo & Kyngas, 2008). However, the researcher kept an open mind when interviewing participants and also did not try to establish any correlation with prior project management experience. A triangulation approach could lead to a more effective phenomenological qualitative study (Leedy & Ormrod, 2010). This researcher invited a colleague to review the raw data without participant names to obtain agreement on the coding schemes appropriateness.

Quantitative research offered more disadvantages for this researcher in this study. A key disadvantage of quantitative research was a researcher must almost be an expert mathematician to posses the skills for statistical analysis (Gaobo & Mark, 2008). Another disadvantage of quantitative research was the black and white approach in explaining data with no gray area (Gaobo & Mark, 2008). For example, the results either proved a theory or did not. Audience members may not be completely satisfied with a "yes" or "no" answer but planned for further understanding of the phenomenon (Willis, 2007).

Therefore, qualitative research method was the right approach for this study. Qualitative phenomenological research included seeking a phenomenon (Shank, 2006). Qualitative phenomenological research contained information on the whole picture of a research problem by a 360 degree view because each participant offered a different perspective (Neuman, 2006). The main objective of this qualitative phenomenological study was to discover common themes of why IT projects failed in pharmaceutical companies by analyzing the data (Leedy & Ormrod, 2010). Because little research materials were available specifically to IT projects in pharmaceutical organizations, qualitative phenomenological research can help identify the phenomenon (Willis, 2007).

This qualitative phenomenological research goals' included discovery and understanding why IT projects failed so often in pharmaceutical companies by analyzing data from the first-hand experiences of participants. Qualitative research was useful for identifying and understanding the phenomenon of IT projects failures (Ojiako et al., 2008). The current study contained an exploration into the diverse experiences of stakeholders, project managers, and project team members who were directly involved in project management tasks of IT projects, by providing them an opportunity to answer open-ended research questions (Willis, 2007).

On the other hand, quantitative research was a good choice for this study. Quantitative research involved studying relationships between dependent and independent variables (Leedy & Ormrod, 2010). Because there was not a complete understanding of why IT projects fail during literature review, no credible variables can be identified at the time. The purpose of this qualitative phenomenological study was not to establish relationships between variables, but to explore first-hand accounts of the participants to reach recommendations or a phenomenon theory (Neuman, 2006).

Qualitative phenomenological research design was a solid choice for this study because researcher tried to understand the participants' perspectives on the failed IT projects (Leedy & Ormod, 2010). By looking at diverse perspectives of the failed IT projects, common themes can emerge from the analysis of data (Neuman, 2006). The unstructured or informal interview approach of a phenomenological study may relax the participants, so they can be more open to the interviewer and provide an honest perspective (Shank, 2006). Popular qualitative research designs included (a) case study, (b) ethnography, (c) grounded theory study, (d) content analysis, and (e) phenomenological study. The goal of this study was to explore the first-hand lived perspectives of the participants on failed IT projects phenomenon. The next few sections explained why the above mentioned qualitative research designs were appropriate for this study, and why phenomenological study was the best research resign for this study.

Case study research design was about researching a particular IT project or program (Leedy & Ormrod, 2010). Also case study involved studying a project over time (Neuman, 2006). In this study, the goal was for the researcher to look at many projects across many types of programs. Furthermore, once a project reached closure, there was no reason to review it over time. Therefore, case study was not appropriate for this study.

Ethnography research design involved studying a group of the same culture or similar community (Neuman, 2006). Also ethnography focused on in-depth social interaction behaviors such as languages and customs (Leedy & Ormrod, 2010). Ethnography research design was not appropriate for this study after that the participants came from different companies and cultures, and the focus was not on any social aspect of the participants (Leedy & Ormrod, 2010; Neuman, 2006).

Grounded theory research design included development of a new theory to explain the phenomenon (Shank, 2006). Grounded theory was an analysis of qualitative data to develop a tentative theory of why IT projects failed regularly (Willis, 2007). The purpose of this study was not to explore a new theory, which would be a grounded theory study and not appropriate (Leedy & Ormrod, 2010).

Content analysis involved a detailed examination on the forms of communications such as e-mails, video tapes, and publications (Leedy & Ormrod, 2010). Due to confidentiality nature of the study, the participants did not and cannot share any written documents from their employers without permission. Therefore, content analysis was not appropriate because of unavailability of materials to review.

Phenomenological study included an exploration of the first-hand experiences of the participants where the participants' perceptions and lived experiences were recorded and analyzed (Willis, 2007). Phenomenological study depended on lengthy interviews to develop an understanding of the phenomenon, and this study's intent was to use interviews (Neuman, 2006). The use of phenomenology can aid in the understanding of the problems why IT projects failed (Leedy & Ormrod, 2010). The phenomenological design was appropriate because this study required analyzing participants in various phases of an IT project and from different organizations (Shank, 2006). Therefore, phenomenological study was the most appropriate method for this research.

Population, Sampling, Data Collection Procedure and Rationale

Population and Rationale

The population of this study was the stakeholders, project managers, and project team members who had first-hand experience with failed IT projects in pharmaceutical organizations. This study included 15 participants from the Research Triangle Park, North Carolina area. The pharmaceutical organizations were companies that contained representatives in the Research Triangle Park area. Because the researcher was local to Research Triangle Park, selecting this area would cut down on travel cost associated with the interviewing process. Furthermore, follow-up meetings should be easier to arrange than long distance arrangements. The goal was to reach data saturation with the 15 participants. Data saturation occurred when there was repetition of common themes and no introduction of new themes (Leedy & Ormrod, 2010).

Sample Size and Rationale

Qualitative data collection used a small sample size, and the questions were open-ended (Shank, 2006). Unlike quantitative research, qualitative researchers may not have data on a new phenomenon and must use face-to-face or phone interviews to collect this new data (Shank, 2006). A qualitative researcher may develop relationships with the participants in the study because of the nature of the collection of data. The researcher was the primary instrument for data collection in qualitative research (Shank, 2006). The effort to collect data via a qualitative approach was time-consuming so, researchers often considered use of a small sample size (Leedy & Ormrod, 2010).

This effort was a qualitative study (not quantitative), so the sample size outlined a focus on smaller size to permit for a detailed discussion during each interview (Willis, 2007). The sample size of this study included 15 stakeholders, project managers, and project team members from failed IT projects in pharmaceutical organizations. Qualitative researchers contained different preferences for the correct amount of sample sizes (Neuman, 2006). A typical size for a phenomenological study was between five to 25 individuals, and this study involved 15 participants which were within the recommended range (Leedy & Ormrod, 2010). Seeking too many samples may not permit for a detailed interview; but having too few samples will not permit data saturation either (Shank, 2006).

Sampling and Rationale

The process of selecting the participants was sampling. Qualitative researchers were purposeful in their selections of participants, so random sampling was not used (Leedy & Ormrod, 2010). The point was to select participants who had the most first-hand experiences on IT projects that failed by using purposive and deviant case sampling methods.

Purposive and deviant case sampling methods were appropriate for this study. Purposive sampling method aided in identification of participants with first-hand experiences in the IT project management failure experience (Willis, 2007). Deviant case sampling involved studying extreme examples of failed IT projects (Neuman, 2006). The goal was to discover IT projects that were infamously deficient from the perspectives of stakeholders, project managers, and project team members. The participant pool consisted of organizational members with direct involvement in the failed IT projects.

The pool of candidates for this research study came from the Project Management Institute (PMI) chapter of Raleigh, North Carolina. From previous attendance at PMI meetings, this researcher noticed that chapter memberships included stakeholders, project managers, and other project team members. Purposive sampling was used to pick candidates who had first-hand or lived experiences of failed IT projects in pharmaceutical industry. After identification of these candidates by purposive sampling, the next step was to use deviant case sampling to find extreme cases of project failures until researcher reached 15 participants (Leedy & Ormrod, 2010). Extreme case examples were projects that failed so miserably that set a new standard for failure in that organization. An example project that finished very late, extremely over budget and of low quality would be a good outcome of deviant case sampling. Purposive and deviant case samplings permitted the researcher to select which participants can help the researcher to understand the situation completely (Neuman, 2006).

Informed Consent, Confidentiality, and Setting

Informed Consent

This study required an informed consent, so the participants were fully aware of the study, including any potential risks (Willis, 2007). The researcher was ethically and morally responsible for the study and thus the participants (Leedy & Ormrod, 2010). The informed consent can be found in Appendix A. One goal of the informed consent was to permit the participants to participate at will, and the data was confidential and protected (Shank, 2006).

Participants were informed that no monetary value will be given for participation and no negative consequences if participants refused to participate. Researcher did not weigh a participant's high rank or profile (ex. Vice President) above others; all participants were equal in status for this study.

Potential participants received the informed consent up to four weeks prior to the scheduled interview dates. To ensure confidentiality, the participants were provided with self-addressed stamped envelopes that can be sent directly to researcher via US Postal Service mail. No fax number were provided since submission by fax may lead to confidentiality breach because fax machines were usually located in open, easily accessible areas, and faxes came in unsealed. Any individual failing to sign the informed consent form was not a participant in the study.

Confidentiality

A high priority of this study was to maintain the confidentiality and privacy of the participants. Researcher informed the participants on the steps taken to ensure protection prior to interviewing. No personal identification data such as birth date, social security number, and employee number were collected. Interviews were conducted in a closed-door environment to maintain confidentiality. A closed-door environment can help a participant relax and aid in remembering more details about what went wrong with the projects instead of being distracted by noise or other people (Leedy & Ormrod, 2010). This researcher discussed the information from the interview with only that participant and not any other participants. During transit from interview location to the researcher's home, the data was kept in a locked briefcase, and the briefcase locked in a car. Interview data was kept in a locked cabinet in the researcher's home, and the home had an active security system. All collected data will be personally shredded by the researcher one year after publication of this study.

Pseudonym Designation

To ensure anonymity, each participant received a pseudonym designation (Participant 001, Participant 002, Participant 003, etc.…). Their names and their companies' names were not listed in the data. Assigning number designation was a recommended approach for qualitative researchers (Leedy & Ormrod, 2010). The data was stored in a locked cabinet in the home of the researcher where only he had the key to open.

Geographic Setting

This study took place in Research Triangle Park, North Carolina. Research Triangle Park was home to more than 500 biotechnology, pharmaceutical and life sciences companies while employing almost 60,000 employees (Carolina Chamber of Commerce, 2012). The state of North Carolina consistently ranked in the top five states for pharmaceutical drug development in the US (Carolina Chamber of Commerce, 2012). Conveniently, Research Triangle Park was also home to this researcher, so most pharmaceutical corporations were within 30-minute driving distance for interviews.

Data Collection Pilot

After Institution Review Board approval, researcher conducted a pilot test to verify the efficacy of the data collection plan. Data collected from the pilot tests will were not used for the study. A pilot study was appropriate for trying out the interview procedure, measurement instruments, and method of analysis (Leedy & Ormrod, 2010). This pilot study permitted the researcher to fine-tune the data collection process.

Data Collection

Data Collection Techniques

Qualitative data collection used a small sample size, and the questions were open-ended (Shank, 2006). Unlike quantitative research, qualitative researchers may not have data on a new phenomenon and must use face-to-face or phone interviews to collect this new data (Shank, 2006). A qualitative researcher often developed working relationships with the participants in the study because of the nature of the collection of data. The researcher was the main instrument for data collection in qualitative research (Shank, 2006). The effort to collect data via a qualitative approach was time-consuming, so only a small sample size was used (Leedy & Ormrod, 2010).

Appropriate data collection techniques in qualitative research included (a) face-to-face, (b) telephone or cellular, and (c) e-mail interviews (Leedy & Ormrod, 2010). Face-to-face interviewing was the preferred interview method for this study because of the close proximity between participants and the researcher. However, telephone and e-mail interviews would still be appropriate due to circumstances beyond control of participants or researcher (Willis, 2007).

Interview Techniques

The main purpose of qualitative phenomenological research was to uncover the phenomenon of the subject under exploration (Neuman, 2006). Semi-structured interviewing process was used because each participant brings a different perspective which may require additional questions tailored to a participant (Leedy & Ormrod, 2010). Open-ended questions permitted participants to expand on their experiences of why they thought IT projects continue to fail at a high rate (Willis, 2007).

This researcher used semi-structured, face-to-face or over-the-telephone interviews with stakeholders, project managers, and project team members in Research Triangle Park, North Carolina. No interviews were conducted without confirmation of signature on informed consent by participants. The interviews were scheduled at the convenience of each participant and conducted at locations appropriate for confidential interviewing. The interviews were at different locations throughout the Research Triangle Park. All participants must grant permissions for the interviews to be recorded, or they will not participate. The purpose of the recording was to ensure the researcher did not misunderstand the message and can follow up for clarification if required. Research participants shared their perspectives on why they thought the IT projects they were involved with failed.

Once interview notes and recordings were transcribed, the researcher requested the participants to review the transcript for correctness. Only this researcher had access to notes and recordings of the interviews, and the materials were kept in a secured location. The results of the study were posted anonymously, so the participants and their organizations were protected.

Types of Data to Be Collected

The collected data were from one or a combination of three sources: (a) interview data and recordings from 15 stakeholders, project managers, and project team members, (b) observations, and (c) non-confidential documents and records. Non-confidential documents or records were publicly accessible and should not situate a participant to be at risk. The researcher relied mostly on the data collected from the face-to-face interviews because a live-meeting increased accuracy (Shank, 2006).

Instrument Appropriateness and Reliability

The primary research question was why did information technology projects continue to fail at over 72% in pharmaceutical companies. The four sub-research questions used in this study guided the interviews by permitting the participants to discuss in details. Research questions permitted focus to the purpose of the study (Neuman, 2006). The use of open-ended questions permitted the participants to expand on their experiences on failed IT projects to find the phenomenon (Willis, 2007). To reach the objective of understanding why IT projects failed in pharmaceutical organizations, this study included the following research questions to organize the study:

RQ1: What factors cause information technology projects to continue failing at a high rate?

RQ2: What effect does project management software such as Microsoft Project have on project failures?

RQ3: What leadership characteristics do successful project managers have?

RQ4: What effect does PMI training and certification of project managers have on failure experiences?

Appendix B contained the interview questions derived from the research questions above. The researcher used the interview questions to organize and facilitate the interviewing process (Leedy & Ormrod, 2010). Answers from the interview questions aided the researcher in understanding what caused IT projects to fail (Willis, 2007).

Reliability and Validity

Reliability and validity in qualitative research translated to accuracy and credibility of the study (Leedy & Ormrod, 2010). Also validity indicated consistency and honesty of research, so a researcher can defend the results (Neuman, 2006). This study included internal and external validity.

Reliability

The research questions combined to form an instrument to help understand why participants think IT projects failed. Data triangulation was used to ensure reliability by collecting data from different time, space, and person (Polit & Beck, 2008). Triangulation was another mean to ensure reliability and reducing limitations of research design (Neuman, 2006). Triangulation can increase the credibility of this study (Leedy & Ormrod, 2010). Interviews conducted on different dates (time), in different companies (space), and with perspectives from different groups of stakeholders, project managers, and project team members (person).

Internal Validity

The main purpose of internal validity was to reduce or eliminate other possible explanation (Leedy & Ormrod, 2010). A researcher should be able to reproduce the results (Willis, 2007). To eliminate internal validity, this researcher disregarded any previous experience from project management to reduce bias (Neuman, 2006).

External Validity

External validity referred to the reproduction of results in another context (Leedy & Ormrod, 2010). However, the purpose of this study was to examine participants specific to Research Triangle Park, North Carolina and specific to pharmaceutical companies. Therefore, a limitation existed on generalization.

Data Analysis

Leedy and Ormrod (2010) stated that researchers should follow these steps for a qualitative data analysis (p. 142):

1. Transcribe the data from the face to face interviews. Entering the raw data into electronic media such as Microsoft Word and Excel.
2. Identify statements that addressed the research topic. Researcher searched for key words and phrases.
3. Group statements into categories that offer meanings to phenomenon. Provided group headings to repeated themes discovered during analysis.
4. Explore contradictory perspectives. Tried to understand why different participants gave paradox statements. Maybe follow up with participants to ensure they meant what they stated.
5. Construct a composite to identify common themes. Sought to identify correlations on combinations of key words and phrases and group the similarities together in a matrix.

Transcribing the data included entering raw data and converting and editing to an appropriate format (Neuman, 2006). Coding and categorizing the data were essential, so the researcher was not overwhelmed with information that contained no relationship of meaning (Willis, 2007). nVivo 10 software was used to make the data analysis phase easier to identify themes (Shank, 2006).

Another approach, a qualitative researcher could use the four steps in qualitative data analysis include these ideas (Shank, 2006, p. 146):

1. Deciding what type of analysis to use. Kept analyzing until saturation or no new themes discovered.
2. Classifying data already collected. Grouped common themes together.
3. Developing relationships between the different types of data. Explored the correlations between the data.
4. Presenting the results of analysis. Triangulated to ensure reliability.

To aid in qualitative data analysis, researchers used thematic analysis which was the "process of understanding qualitative data analysis is to explore the art and practice of coding and analyzing from a more traditionally scientific perspective" (Shank, 2006, p. 148). Finally, qualitative researchers must focus on reliability, validity, and generalizability of the analysis (Shank, 2006, p. 148). Qualitative research focused less on the significance of coding and categorizing of data than quantitative research (Shank, 2006).

Summary

Chapter 3 included an explanation of the methodology of the current qualitative phenomenological study to explore the first-hand experiences of stakeholders, project managers, and project team members to examine why IT projects continued to fail at a high-rate in pharmaceutical companies. The use of qualitative research permitted better understanding of the big picture problem of IT projects failures (Leedy & Ormrod, 2010). Phenomenological study permitted participants to expand on their first-hand experiences on these failures (Neuman, 2006).

Chapter 3 outlined and described selection of participants, instrumentation, data collection, and data analysis. Purposive and deviant case sampling methods were used to select 15 stakeholders, project managers, and project team members from pharmaceutical companies in

Research Triangle Park, North Carolina (Leedy & Ormrod, 2010). The current study involved data collection sources of (a) interviews, (b) observations, and (c) non-confidential documents. A qualitative software tool, nVivo 10, was used to expedite trending analysis of the collected data. Chapter 4 contained information on the data analysis from participants' interviews and the results of that analysis.

Chapter 4: Analysis and Results

The general problem addressed in this qualitative phenomenological study was the high failure rate of IT projects in pharmaceutical industry (PMI, 2009). The specific problem addressed was the lack of understanding about the reasons why the continued high rate of IT projects failures (Cerpa & Verner, 2009). The study involved examination of leadership models and theories. Leadership models and theories included (a) Frederick Taylor's scientific management theory, (b) Vroom-Yetton Jago decision model, (c) Rogers' diffusion of innovation theory, (d) Henri Fayol's management theory, and (e) Douglas McGregor's Theory X and Y (Weiyin, Thong, Chasalow, & Dhillon, 2011).

The data collection involved in-person and over-the-phone interviews with15 stakeholders, project managers, and project team members who had first-hand experiences in failed IT projects in pharmaceutical industry located in or conducting business in Research Triangle Park, North Carolina. A failed IT project was a project that did not complete on time, within budget, or with quality. Stakeholders, project managers, and project team members included vice presidents, various directors of information technology, project managers, developers, testers, programmers, and business analysts.

The researcher interviewed each participant either in person or over the telephone for up to one hour time period. This phenomenological tactic permitted themes to surface from the 15 participants. Answers provided insight into why did IT projects continue to fail at a high rate.

Organization of Chapter 4

Chapter 4 contained a description of the sampling methods, pilot testing, data collection procedures, and results of data analysis. The chapter 4 framework was based on the research questions in chapter 1, and the research approach explained in chapter 3. To highlight, chapter 4 included the following sections: (a) research approach review, (b) sampling method, (c) pilot testing, (d) research questions, (e) the data collection steps, (f) data analysis, (g) findings, (h) questionable data, and (i) chapter 4 summary. Chapter 4 finished with presentation of the research findings that materialized from the 15 phenomenological interviews performed for the study. The results of the findings showcased emerging themes on why IT projects continue to fail at a high rate.

Synopsis of the Problem Statement

The failure rate of IT projects was greater than 72% (PMI, 2009). In 2007, the Standish Group reported IT projects success rate were only at 35% (Cerpa & Verner, 2009). In 2011, project success was up slightly to 37% ("Failure rates finally drop," 2011). The high failure rate delayed drug development. People were dependent on drugs to cure troublesome diseases and other major ailments. Some people even depended on drugs to save their lives or the lives of loved ones. Drug development was not fast enough because many factors led to delays in launching new drug products such as IT projects (Kaitin, 2010). A delay in drug launch set back a company on average $15 million per day on each drug (Noffke, 2007). Drug launch delay (a) diminished a company's ability to earn back research and development cost, (b) left door open for competition to release their versions of similar drugs, and (c) left patients waiting for safe drug treatment options (Noffke, 2007). One critical factor was the IT projects that support drug development were constantly taking longer than expected (Civan & Maloney, 2009).

A report by PMI stated poor project management and implementation skills were two key factors in project failures (PMI, 2009). Failures in information technology projects delayed the delivery of drugs to patients which needed the drugs to get better and live longer (PMI, 2009). The problem was that information technology projects in pharmaceutical companies continue to fail because of (a) finishing late, (b) over-budget, or with (c) low quality causing delays in drug development to save people's lives. For example, Pfizer Pharmaceutical's Lipitor cholesterol drug delay would cost the company $35 million per day (Noffke, 2007). The latest report showed 42 million Americans suffered from high cholesterol, and this drug delay would limit their treatment choices (WebMD, 2012). Drug development cost on only one drug could be as high as $2 billion, so drug companies were eager to recoup drug cost quickly (Mikhail & Giddings, 2011).

Synopsis of the Research Method

The current study represented a phenomenological research design within a qualitative research method. As the objective of this current study was to analyze the IT projects failures phenomenon through the first-hand experiences of 15 project team members and stakeholders who participated with the projects, a phenomenological research design was suitable for the current qualitative study. Qualitative was appropriate over quantitative for this study because the focus was to answer "why" projects were continuing to fail at a high rate (Leedy & Ormrod, 2010). IT projects were unique, had clear starts and end dates, and added functionalities to hardware, software, or network infrastructure pieces (PMI, 2008). People planned, implemented, and controlled IT projects with focus on formal project management methodology (PMI, 2008). The general population of the current study was the project managers, team members, and stakeholders within the Research Triangle Park, North Carolina pharmaceutical companies. The stakeholders were in positions of authorities in dealing with the project management activities of the IT projects with titles such as Director of Projects, Director of ERP, and Vice President (VP) of IT.

Study Population

The purpose of this qualitative phenomenological study was to explore the perceptions of 15 IT personnel from pharmaceutical companies in Research Triangle Park in Raleigh, North Carolina who witnessed first-hand on what factors caused project failures. Phenomenological research had been a popular qualitative research strategy for the last 20 years (Shank, 2006). Phenomenological research was about the assumption that subjects of research have a conscious for communication (Willis, 2007). Phenomenological research distinguished between noumena or real things and the perceptions of them or phenomena (Willis, 2007, p. 172). Therefore, phenomenological research focused on consciousness and perception (Neuman, 2006). The main task of phenomenological research was identifying common themes in people's descriptions of their own perceptions on how the projects failed (Leedy & Ormrod, 2010). Researchers obtained data for phenomenological research by interviewing and questioning participants (Willis, 2007). A researcher's goal was to understand the participants' experiences and perceptions of the situation (Leedy & Ormrod, 2010).

Sampling Method

Purposive and deviant case sampling methods were appropriate for this study. Purposive sampling method aided in identification of participants with first-hand experiences in the IT project management failure experience (Willis, 2007). Deviant case sampling resulted in extreme examples of failed IT projects (Neuman, 2006). The goal was to discover IT projects that were infamously deficient from the perspectives of stakeholders, project managers, and project team members. The participant pool consisted of employees of pharmaceutical companies with direct involvement in the failed IT projects.

The pool of candidates for this research study came from the Project Management Institute (PMI) chapter in Research Triangle Park (RTP), North Carolina. From previous attendance at PMI meetings, this researcher noticed that chapter memberships included stakeholders, project managers, and other project team members. Purposive sampling was used to pick candidates who have first-hand or lived experiences of failed IT projects in pharmaceutical industry. After identification of these candidates by purposive sampling, the next step was to use deviant case sampling to find extreme cases of project failures until researcher reached 15 participants (Leedy & Ormrod, 2010). Extreme case examples were projects that failed so dejectedly that people often referenced the failure in that organization. For example, a project that finished very late, exceedingly over budget and of low quality would be a good outcome of deviant case sampling. Purposive and deviant case samplings permitted the researcher to select which participants can help the researcher understand the situation completely (Neuman, 2006). There was a chance that participants may be embarrassed by their actions leading to failed IT projects and would not tell a complete picture. This researcher granted the participants confidentiality and privacy protection to encourage them to speak the truth.

The Project Management Institute (PMI) RTP Chapter President introduced the researcher and research topic at the May and June 2012 monthly chapter meetings. Researcher provided contact information for potential participants who would like to participate in the study. Researcher accepted the first 17 participants who called or emailed that met the research requirements. After the first 17, this researcher informed the next round of participants that they will be put on a wait-list in case any of the first 17 participants could not fulfill their participation duties.

The 17 candidates received an email from this researcher asking them formally to participate in the study (please see Appendix A). Of the 17 candidates, 12 replied indicating their continued interest in the study, and four did not respond. Researcher used deviant case sampling methods and called the next set of participants to select four additional participants that experienced examples of IT projects failing despondently in pharmaceutical companies. Researcher stopped contacting other participants after confirming 17 participants willingly to proceed with interviews.

Research and Interview Questions

Appendix C contained the qualitative phenomenological interview questions that the 17 participants answered. The questions supported research into the main research question of why did IT projects continue to fail at a high rate and four research questions. The questions below permitted further examination and better understanding of the IT projects failure phenomenon:

RQ1: What factors cause information technology projects to continue failing at a high rate?

RQ2: What effect does project management software such as Microsoft Project have on project failures?

RQ3: What leadership characteristics do successful project managers have?

RQ4: What effect does PMI training and certification of project managers have on failure experiences?

Data Collection Pilot Study

To determine the effectiveness or efficacy of this data collection procedure, researcher conducted a pilot test with the first two participants who met the study requirements after the approval of Internal Review Board (IRB). The data collected showed the reliability of the interview and data collection processes. This first two participants' data were not used in the study because the pilot's purpose was to aid in tweaking the data collection process. Findings from the pilot included that (a) the interview completed within the time scope of one hour, (b) questions were clear and simple enough for understanding without much clarification needed, (c) interview process was self-contained by not needing additional tools.

The Pilot Study

The two participants for the pilot test were the first available to the researcher out of all the participants. The pilot participants had project management experience with a failed IT projects in pharmaceutical industry. The two pilot participants averaged 15 years of industry experience with a four-year college degree each.

The Pilot Study Results

Both pilot interviews took less than 1 hour, which was the time limit for the interview. The pilot participants recommended providing more details to the questions. The pilot participants also asked to have the questions in advance, so they could recollect more details from their memories to provide answers. Here was a summary of what the pilot participants recommended and taken into consideration:

1. Provide interview questions prior to meeting. One pilot participant stated that participants usually have many real-life examples, and provided the questions in advance may permit other participants to think of the most appropriate or best responses.
2. Introduction. The participants suggested a reminder of the study because even though they read the consent form and purpose of study, they may forgotten by the interview

time. This introduction kept the interview within scope of the study, otherwise it may veer to a different path.

3. Definition. Participants would like to make sure they were in alignment with researcher on the definition of project failure. The definition of project failure in this case was a project that (a) finished late, (b) over-budget, and/or (c) with poor quality.
4. Examples. Participants would like examples of what kind of answers the researcher was looking for. Without providing examples, the participants felt lost in discussing the topic.
5. Reminder of confidentiality. The participants were a little hesitant to answer questions that referenced other people or their own failures. However, when the researcher reminded them that this study was completely confidential, they began to open up more and provided better examples.

In summary, only minor tweaks were made to the interview questions and study process because the participants were able to provide answers based on experience within the time limit. The results of these two pilot participants were not used in the study. The researcher must maintain focus with the participants or the interviews will venture to different paths quickly. Finally, this researcher reminded them of scope of study and full confidentiality.

Data Collection Process

This researcher collected interview data from 15 participants in the Research Triangle Park, NC area after IRB approval. The first interview started in June 2012 and the last interview was in August 2012. Participants received and signed informed consent and confidentiality agreements (Appendix A) prior to the researcher setting up an interview. The participants understood that they voluntary participated and their responses were recorded. Furthermore, the participants valued the fact that their data were kept confidential. Only the researcher knew the names of the participants. This researcher reserved a small, closed door conference room at the Cary Library in Cary, North Carolina for interviews to increase comfort and minimize interruptions.

Researcher made every effort to conduct interviews face-to-face; however, a couple of interviews were conducted over the phone because of personal issues with participants on the days of interviews. Phone interviewing for phenomenological study was a valuable date collection technique, and researchers should not rely entirely on face-to-face interviews (Sweet, 2002). In some qualitative phenomenological studies, researchers used more phone interviews than face-to-face interviews because of challenges for the participants to meet in person (Alnaser, 2009). Researchers did not see any disadvantages affecting their studies by using phone over face-to-face interviews (Standing, 2011).

Participants' Profiles

The researcher's role was to maintain confidentiality of each participant. This researcher used the coding process highlighted in Table 2 above. The designations were the participants' profiles at the time of the failed projects.

1. Participant 001 was a project manager with 12 years work experience. Achieved a bachelor degree and was a certified PMP. Participant is a male.
2. Participant 002 was a female project manager with 15 years work experience. Achieved a bachelor degree but was not a PMP at time of failed project.
3. Participant 003 was a project manager with 20 years work experience. Participant achieved a bachelor degree and was a certified PMP. Participant is a male.

4. Participant 004 was a stakeholder with 25 years experience at time of failed project. Participant 004 completed some college work but did not achieve graduation status. Participant is female and not a PMP.
5. Participant 005 was a stakeholder with 23 years experience. Participant is male and completed three years of college coursework at time of failed project. Participant was not a PMP.
6. Participant 006 was a team member of a failed project. Participant had 15 years of experience with a bachelor degree. Participant is male and did not have PMP.
7. Participant 007 had 19 years of experience and a team member of failed project. Participant had a bachelor degree but no PMP certification. Participant is male.
8. Participant 008 was a stakeholder with 28 years of experience. Participant is male with a bachelor degree. Participant did not hold PMP certification.
9. Participant 009 was a team member with 30 years of experience. Participant had a master's degree but no PMP. Participant is male.
10. Participant 010 was a team member with 20 years experience. Participant had a bachelor degree. Participant is male and held PMP certification at time of failed project.
11. Participant 011 was a stakeholder with a bachelor degree. Participant also obtained a PMP certification and is male.
12. Participant 012 was a project manager with 18 years experience. Participant had no PMP but achieved a bachelor degree. Participant is male.
13. Participant 013 was a stakeholder on a failed project. Participant had masters and PMP certification. Participant is male and had 20 years of experience.

14. Participant 014 was a project manager with 15 years of experience. Participant is male with master's degree. Participant also had PMP certification.
15. Participant 015 had a bachelor degree with 12 years of experience. Participant is female and had no PMP certification. Participant was a team member on a failed project.

Demographic Data

Before discussion of the demographic data, Table 2 contained explanation and definition for each role header. The purpose of collection of demographic data was to understand what types of candidates were in the study. The goal was to seek diversification in the participants' pool. Primary concern was for the protection of participant's identification, so only pseudonyms were used for tagging participants in the study.

Table 2

Designation Scheme for Coding Each Participant

Participant Identification	Use pseudonym instead of participants' real name to protect confidentiality. Ex. Participant 001, Participant 002, etc....
Role	One of three roles for the participants during the failed project. The roles were Stakeholder, Project Manager, or Team Member
Years of Professional Experience	Number of years of professional working experience of the participants at time of failed

	project
Education	Education level of participants at time of failed project
PMI Certification Status	At time of failed project, was participant a certified Project Management Professional (PMP) by Project Management Institute (PMI)
Gender	Male or Female

The 15 study participants were project managers, stakeholders, or team members at the time of the failed projects from the Research Triangle Park, North Carolina area. The researcher selected participants from different age groups and experience years. The participants worked at different pharmaceutical companies at different points in time. The participants also represented different genders and academic achievement levels. Participants received pseudonyms to maintain privacy and confidentiality. Table 3 provided a summary of the demographics of the 15 participants.

Table 3

Summary of the Demographic Data

Participant	Role	Years of Professional Experience	Education	Gender	Project Management Certification
001	Project Manager	12	Bachelor	Male	Yes
002	Project	15	Bachelor	Female	No

	Manager				
003	Project Manager	20	Bachelor	Male	Yes
004	Stakeholder	25	Some College	Female	No
005	Stakeholder	23	Some College	Male	No
006	Team Member	15	Bachelor	Male	No
007	Team Member	19	Bachelor	Male	No
008	Stakeholder	28	Bachelor	Male	No
009	Team Member	30	Masters	Male	No
010	Team Member	20	Bachelor	Male	Yes
011	Stakeholder	17	Bachelor	Male	Yes
012	Project Manager	18	Bachelor	Male	No
013	Stakeholder	20	Masters	Male	Yes
014	Project Manager	15	Masters	Male	Yes
015	Team Member	12	Bachelor	Female	No

Table 4 showed the distribution of the three key roles for this study. There were five representatives from each group of stakeholders, project managers, and team members. This distribution permitted diversity of experiences. This researcher used purposive and deviant case samplings to pick an equal distribution of the roles. This equal distribution permitted a balance and 360 degree view of the key players in failed IT projects (Leedy & Ormrod, 2010).

Table 4

Role Distribution

Role	**Frequency**	**Percentage**
Project Manager	5	33%
Stakeholder	5	33%
Team Member	5	33%

Table 5 showed the distribution of the years of professional experience. The distribution indicated an experience working group of participants. Most acquired 11 to 15 and 16 to 20 years of working experience. No participants had less than 10 years of experience.

One can rule out lack of professional experience or rookie status as reason for project failure because the participants had double-digit years of experience.

Table 5

Years of Experience Distribution

Years of Professional Experience	Frequency	Percentage
Less than 10	0	0%
11 to 15	5	33%
16 to 20	6	40%
21 to 25	2	13%
26 to 30	2	13%

Table 6 showed the distribution for academic achievements in education. Most of the participants had a bachelor degree. Three participants gained Masters' degrees. The interpretation here was that the participants were an educated group.

Table 6

Education Distribution

Education	Frequency	Percentage
Some College	2	13%
Bachelor	10	67%
Masters	3	20%

Table 7 showed the gender distribution. Participants were both males and females. Ratio of women to men working in the information technology field was around 16% female in the US (Durante, Griskevicius, Simpson, Cantú, & Tybur, 2012). This study was 20% female, so the ratio was a very close mirroring of the real-world information technology field.

Table 7

Gender Distribution

Gender	Frequency	Percentage
Female	3	20%
Male	12	80%

Table 8 showed the distribution in Project Management Institute (PMI) certifications as a Project Management Professional (PMP). This distribution was almost even, which was fit for purpose in this study because the researcher wanted to obtain opinions from both certified project leaders and non-certified project leaders.

Table 8

PMP Certification Distribution

PMP Certification?	Frequency	Percentage
Yes	6	40%
No	9	60%

The distribution data of the participants of the above tables confirmed validation based on diversification of the roles, years of professional experience, education levels, genders, and PMP certifications. This diversification would lead to a balance, well-rounded research study.

Data Saturation

Participants 013, 014, and 015 provided data consistent with data from Participants 001 to 012. The querying in nVivo 10 showed no new themes in Participants 013, 014, and 015 that were not already discussed by Participants 001 to 012. Researcher concluded that saturation was reached because of no new themes.

Data Triangulation

Triangulation assured validity of the research by overcoming limitations and bias (Willis, 2007). A key type of triangulation was data triangulation involving time, space, and people (Leedy & Ormrod, 2010). Triangulation was another mean to ensure reliability and reducing limitations of research design (Neuman, 2006). This study contained data collected from interviewing 15 different participants on different days at dissimilar locations about different types of IT projects.

For this study, triangulation involved analyzing audio recorded data, participants' language, and researcher's personal notes of the interviews. As the participants were answering the questions, the researcher noted if participants seemed nervous or excited about some questions more than others and noted other changes in patterns. For the two phone interviews, this researcher paid more attention to tone of voice of the participants and made notes if the participants paused frequently or spoke quicker for certain interview questions.

Data triangulation was used to ensure reliability by collecting data from different time, person, and space (Polit & Beck, 2008). This researcher collected data over different days and time periods between June and August 2012 (time). There were 15 different participants at different levels at their companies (person) and their perspectives were from different pharmaceutical companies (space). Each participant also shared project failure points at different phases or time in the projects.

Data Analysis

This current study included interpretative phenomenological analysis (IPA) for data analysis. IPA is a qualitative research approach that had been becoming more popular the past 10 to 15 years, and IPA had its root in psychology with recognition of the researcher as the central role of the research study (Pringle, et al, 2011). IPA involved a two-stage analysis process where (1) the researcher described the data then (2) tried to interpret or make sense of it (Pringle, et al, 2011). To make the conversion from the first-stage to the second stage, researcher used the following five steps (Shank, 2006):

---

1. Bracketing and phenomenological reduction. This researcher reviewed recordings of interviews with an open-mind and tried to be as unbiased as possible by temporary suspending any previous knowledge of IT project management.
2. Delineating units of meaning. Researcher created a list of relevance information by scanning for frequency of words. Reducing the number of units made the list more manageable.
3. Clustering of meaning units to form themes. When placing the units of meaning together, significant themes began to emerge because of repetition from other participants.
4. Summarizing each interview. Once several themes emerged, each interview report was scrutinized to form a summary of the key points of each participant's message.
5. Making a composite summary. The interview reports were brought together to examine recurring set of themes and interpreted conclusions were developed from reflections of the data.

Bracketing and Phenomenological Reduction

Bracketing was when a researcher must suspend any prior experience about the topic, so there was no introduction of undue bias (Leedy & Ormrod, 2010). This phenomenological reduction was necessary for the researcher to fully understand what the participants were stating (Leedy & Ormrod, 2010). A few days prior to the interviews, this researcher took a summer vacation from work and did not indulge in any project management activities or related discussions. Most of the activities over these few vacation days were family related and non-work in nature. When the researcher started the interviewing process with the first participant in June 2012, there was no reflection of project work, and the thoughts were mostly about the family summer vacation of the week before.

Delineating Units of Meaning

The researcher used open-ended questions to permit the participants into opening up about their failed IT projects. The researcher also took observational notes on how each participant's body language or facial expressions changed throughout the interviews, as well as, other sensations. Researcher used (a) circle map, (b) tree map, (c) tag cloud, and (d) 3D word frequency querying tools from the nVivo 10 qualitative research software to drill into the interviewing data.

Circle Map

Researchers used circle maps to identify context, and aided in grouping categories or units of meaning (Graham, & Erwin, 2011). Circle maps were popular because researchers appreciated the flexibility and reflective qualities to aid in brainstorming and assessment of a study (Graham, & Erwin, 2011). A circle map in Figure 3 below contained words used by the participants, and the nVivo 10 software contained a function that mapped similar words by connecting them by lines. In the circle map below created by words the participants used, there were heavy concentrations around the right quadrant of the sphere. The right side of the globe contained common words used by the participants including "communicate," "experience," "risks," "issues," and "important." These words were in the transcripts of Participants 001, 002, 003, 004, 005, 006, 007, 008, 009, 010, 011, 012, 013, and 014. There were more concentrations around the words "development" and "certifications." Development in this study was in reference to software development, and Participants 001, 004, 005, 006, 007, 008, 009, 010, 011, 012, and 015 thought that project managers with certifications were better at leading software development projects than non-certified project managers.

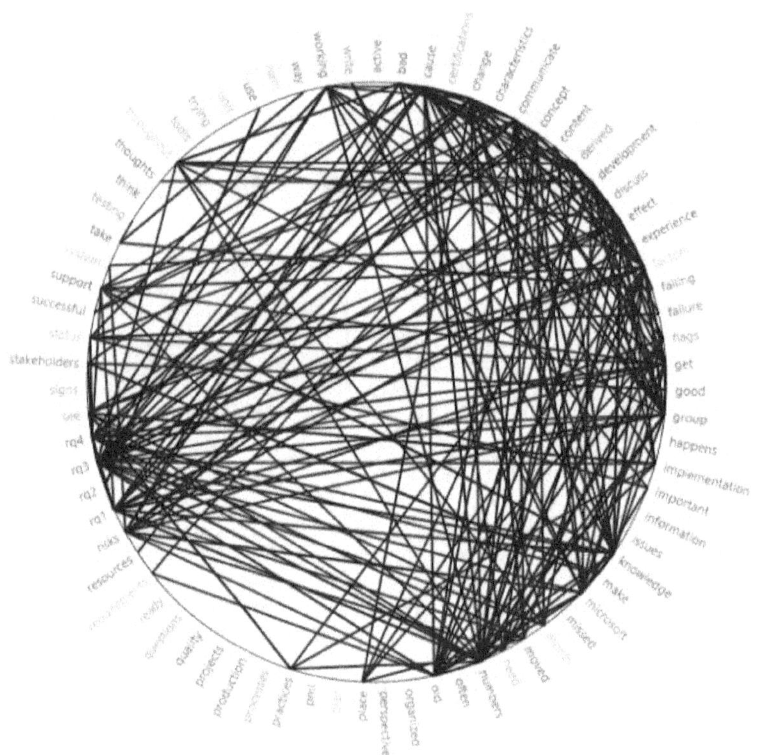

Figure 3: Circle Map of Words the Participants Used in the Interviews

Tree Map

Researchers also used tree maps in classfiying data and development of themes (Ahmad & Alahakoon, 2010). Tree maps aided researchers in identifying themes and sub-themes (Ahmad & Alahakoon, 2010). In the tree map in Figure 4 below, the words "requirements," "thoughts," and "active" were most used by the participants. The word "requirements" was used most often and most frequently. All 15 participants used "requirements" in the interviews. After reviewing the data, "requirements" meant the requirements gathering phase of a project. When project managers and developers tried to understand what they needed to build for the customers, they would conduct requirements gathering. The word "thoughts" meant that the participants personally thought that their projects would fail long before the official announcements. Fifteen participants stated they knew the projects were going to fail. The word "active" meant that participants wished that project managers were more active or pro-active in managing the projects. Thirteen of 15 participants (87%) stated that the projects were in re-active mode most of the time and not pro-active. Participant 003 said, "We were in constant fire fighting mode, always reacting to the next crisis. Since we spent so much time on today's fires, we started missing our next milestones, and tomorrow we would start figuring that out. The point is we were always re-active and not active at managing ahead."

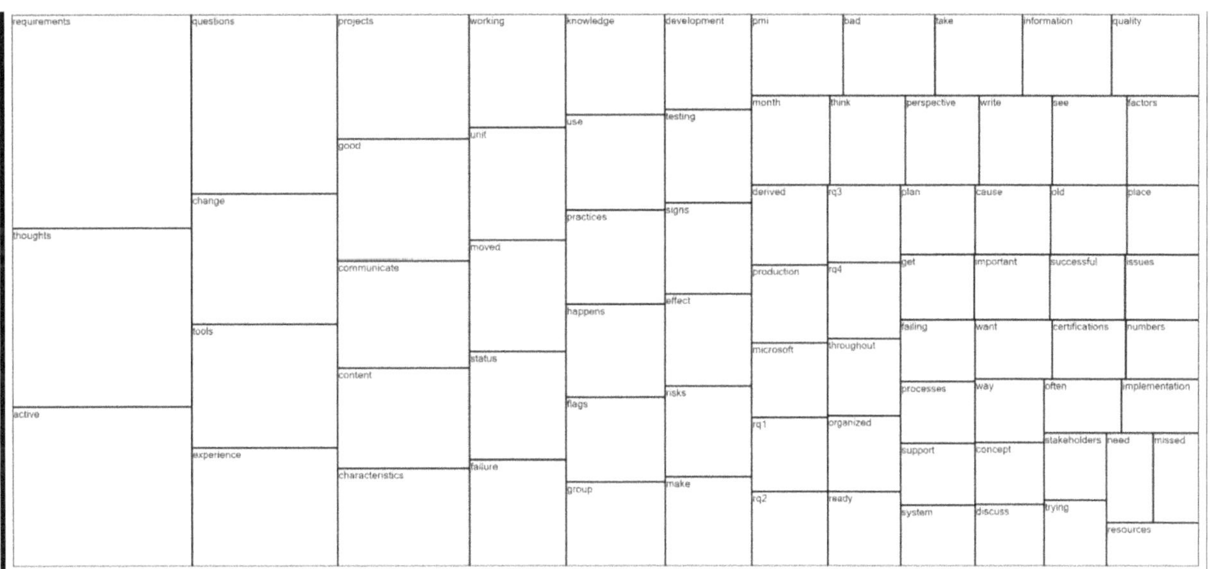

Figure 4: Tree Map of the Participants' Interviews

Tag Cloud

A tag cloud aided researchers in by painting a visual representation of text data, text size increases as word count increases (Gill & Griffin, 2010). In this study, tags were of the 75 most used words by the 15 participants containing more than four characters. Words such as "a," "and," "but," and "the" were eliminated from this tag cloud, and the arrangement was in alphabetical order. Most of the same words stood out again, and by now this researcher saw common themes emerging because of the word views of the research participants' data. Researcher conducted further data analysis because of repetition of several words. The words "change" and "close" came up in the tag cloud, and the researcher reviewed the participants' data for context. The word "change" meant the project kept changing scope without proper change management. The words "close" meant that the project could never close. People kept adding new requirements and deliverables to the project to extend indefinitely. Participant 013 stated, "We did not perform proper change management because we kept adding more work, but never added more time or money. We came so close to finishing the project several times, but as new requirements were added, the project kept getting extended. For example, we were only supposed to add two Oracle database servers: one as primary, and the other as secondary. However, management wanted a second set of servers on the other side of the Atlantic, but refused to consider the extended time."

The words "issues" and "risks" stood out in the tag cloud in Figure 5 below, and this observation was significant because management of issues and risks were critical to proper project management (PMI, 2008). After further data analysis, an interpretation was that on projects that failed the project managers did not manage issues and risks carefully. Participant 004 said, "We did not keep a log of risks or issues, so we had no idea what we needed to worry about. For example, we had a risk that the vendor support contract would expire, but did not document it. In the middle of the project, we lost support of our services and had to scramble to get a new support contract in place. That issue caused our project to delay by one month easily."

Another word that stood out in the tag cloud was "testing." After further data analysis by reviewing the interviews text data, there were insufficient time and resources dedicated to testing. For example, Participant 009 stated, "The project was running late, so we cut down testing cycle to meet the overall project deadline. What once was scoped as complete functional testing is now just kicking the tires testing." Participant 011 stated, "The project manager persuaded the test manager to go ahead and pass testing because the project was in danger of being late. The challenge was that the test manager reported to the project manager, so in a sense, it was a direct order, and the test manager could not fight back."

Figure 5: Tag Cloud of Texts in the Interviews

Word Frequency Count in 3D

Word frequency counter in 3D permitted a researcher to see the most used words easily in visual graphics (Borelli, Sbarra, Mehl, & David, 2011). The words "questions" and "thoughts" stood out in this new perspective of looking at the same data by nVivo 10 in Figure 6 below. Upon further data analysis, the 15 participants had questions about the requirements and directions of their projects. Participants 001, 002, 003, 004, 005, 006, 008, 009, 010, 011, 014, and 015 had "thoughts" that the projects were in trouble but did not know how to escalate or thought someone else would have escalated. Participant 003 said, "I thought the project was in trouble from the early days because the schedule was so aggressive, but I just thought that other people knew what they were doing. I questioned myself several time if the project was in trouble or not." Participant 010 stated, "I began having more and more questions and thoughts on some of the issues we have been seeing, but I assume the other experts would pick up and resolve it before things got too bad."

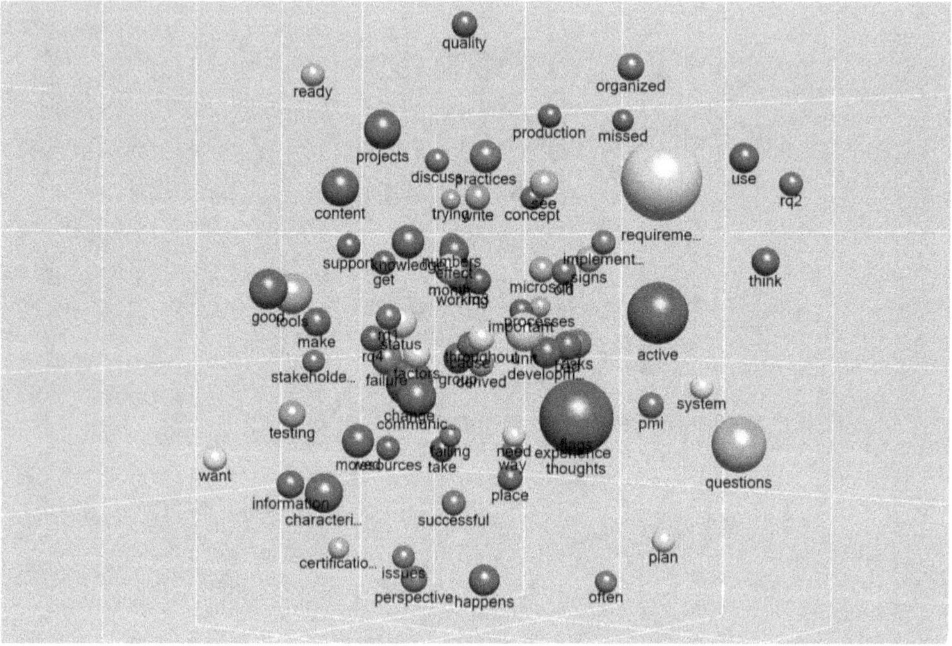

Figure 6: Word Frequency in 3D

Themes and Sub-themes

The phenomenological approach permitted themes and sub-themes to evolve from the 15 participants. Results provided evidence on why IT projects in pharmaceutical companies continue to fail at a high rate. This researcher used the nVivo 10 qualitative software tool to create nodes which led to themes and sub-themes identifications. Themes and sub-themes emerged and listed below.

Table 9

Summary of Themes and Sub-themes

Themes	**Sub-themes**
1) Problems in Requirements Phase	A) Review of requirements
	B) Planning to meet requirements
	C) Setup the project
	D) Initiate the project
2) Problems in Development Phase	A) Lack of communications between team members
	B) No idea of progress
	C) Development work did not match back to requirements
3) Problems in Testing Phase	A) Review of test results
	B) Audit of test cases
	C) Conflict of interest
4) Problems in Deployment / Implementation Phase	A) Customers not ready to accept project
	B) Testing was not sufficient
5) Project Management Tools	A) Tools too complicated
	B) Project Managers did not know how to

	use tools
6) Leadership Characteristics of Project Leaders	Failed projects had project managers who were A) Lazy B) Lack Experience C) Lack of training D) Not flexible E) Not people friendly F) Poor communicator
7) Best Practices in Project Management	A) Kept risks and issues log B) Weekly or daily status reporting C) Follow change management process D) Plan and implement testing without taking shortcuts E) Set a closure date
8) Worst Practices in Project Management	A) Accepted bad test results B) Did not deliver on requirements C) No communications D) Did not manage up to stakeholders
9) Experience Levels of Project Managers	A) More experience project managers were more capable of navigating through issues
10) Certifications of Project Managers	A) Highly trained project managers were

	able to rely on training to get project out of trouble

Theme 1: Problems in Requirements Phase

The requirements gathering phase was usually the first phase of a project (PMI, 2008). Participants stated that the projects already had failure signs at this phase. Failure signs included not careful reviewing or planning of requirements. Even if requirements were fully understood, the projects did not have enough human resources to carry out the development. For example, Participant 006 stated that a database project did not have database experts on the team until later into the project. Fifteen participants (100%) stated they had problems leading to project failures in requirements phase. Problems ranged from poor planning to meet requirements and initiation of the project team to understand requirements according to eight out of 15 participants (53%).

Theme 2: Problems in Development Phase

The projects were finally underway and full development work activities were in-progress, but the project team members had no idea who was working on what. Ten out of 15 participants (67%) cited developers were creating code that did not work or match back to requirements. Nine out of 15 participants (60%) stated a lack of communications during development phase led to project failure. The project managers did not communicate progress, and team members were lost on the direction of their projects. There were misalignments between what developers and engineers designed versus what were in the original business requirements.

Theme 3: Problems in Testing Phase

In the testing phase, testers conducted testing, but there was little review of the test results. Furthermore, no one audited the test cases to ensure that the testing scenarios were fit-for-purpose. Twelve out of 15 participants (80%) stated they had problems with the process for auditing tests. When project time schedule was tight, the project manager forced the test manager or tester to cut back on testing scope. Because the testing team most likely reported up to the project manager in most organizations' reporting structures, there was a conflict of interest in providing testing for a supervising figure of authority. Participant 012 stated that a project manager asked that most of the test cases were removed because the money needed were removed from testers and re-allocated to system developers to cover the over-time pay.

Theme 4: Problems in Deployment / Implementation Phase

Because of insufficient testing, the project was not ready for deployment, but the project manager proceeded anyway. Thirteen of 15 participants (87%) stated they felt the deployment plan did not address risks or issues expected for deployment. Because no mitigation plans were in place, the implementation failed to deploy successfully. There was poor communication with the customers, so they were not ready to accept the project either. When deployed or implemented, the requirements were not met.

Theme 5: Project Management Tools

The project management tools were so complicated that only the project managers knew how to use the tools. Stakeholders and other team members were dependent on the project managers for status reporting. The project managers did not know how to use the tools effectively, and they did not set up red flags function on the tools. Eight of 15 participants (53%) did not know how to properly use project management tools given to them for the project.

Theme 6: Leadership Characteristics of Project Leaders

On projects that failed, the project managers were lazy, lack good experience, not flexible, not people friendly, and considered poor communicators. These characteristics made collaboration with stakeholders and project team members difficult. Several participants stated that a potentially successful project could become a disaster based solely on the ineffectiveness of the project managers. The leading poor characteristic of project managers on failed projects were they did not communicate effectively according to nine out of 15 participants (60%).

Theme 7: Best Practices in Project Management

Participants stated that successful projects most often had good record keeping of risks and issues log, weekly or daily accurate status report, formal change management, testing without taking shortcuts, and closure date defined. The failed projects did not possess most of these best practices activities. The reasons were lack of experience or lack of training and education. Twelve out of 15 participants (80%) said they could not keep up with the constant changing of requirements and scope of work in their projects because lack of formal change management. Thirteen out of 15 participants (87%) stated that project managers were unaware of risks and issues that needed attention.

Theme 8: Worst Practices in Project Management

Participants stated that project managers or stakeholders accepted bad test results because they did not want to miss the deadlines. The failed projects did not have processes to check to make sure people actually delivered on promised requirements. Poor communications led to constant inaccurate and unreliable information, assuming there were communications at all. The stakeholders were not sure on the project status, and escalations took too long to reach people with authority who can take actions. Nine out of 15 participants (60%) were disappointed that project managers proceeded with the project despite bad test results indicating the project team members needed to revisit the defects discovered.

Theme 9: Experience Levels of Project Managers

Participants thought that experienced project managers mitigated many issues and risks that could have made the projects even more disastrous. Rookie or less experienced project managers were not sure how to navigate the projects out of trouble once issues started. Participants thought they saw a correlation between experienced project managers with project success. However, having a seasoned project manager did not guarantee success either. The point was projects failed because the project managers lacked experience in project management. These project managers had strong technical backgrounds, and senior management thought that was good enough to run similar technology projects. Fifteen participants (100%) believed project management experience and education were critical to the project managers' chances for success.

Theme 10: Certifications of Project Managers

Participants thought that highly trained or certified project managers were able to solve problems quicker. The certified project managers had tools and processes at their disposal for just about any project situation. However, highly trained project managers without experience can lead to project failure too.

Making a Composite Summary

In Figure 7 below, this researcher concluded from the data analysis that a project can fail at any phase of the project life cycle. At the first phase of requirements, the participants stated they felt uneasy and had many questions around what the purpose of the projects were. In hindsight, maybe someone should have raised their hands or flags stating their concerns.

However, the members of the project wanted to be good corporate citizens and did not want to come across as holding up progress. Fifteen out of 15 (100%) of the participants felt project teams did not plan enough. When the project was under development, nine out of 15 participants (60%) felt communication was lacking between the team members, and 10 out of 15 participants (67%) questioned if the development work actually mirrored requirements. After completion of development, the testing phase had several challenges that led to project failures. By testing phase, the project was behind schedule and testers were instructed to accept almost any type of test results. Furthermore, the testing was not sufficient, and 13 out of 15 participants (87%) felt a conflict of interest because the people testing were also developers and reported to the project manager. Once the development and testing work were completed, deployment was next. Project can fail at implementation and deployment phase because testing was not sufficient and the customer was not ready to accept the project because of lack of training or lack of communication.

As for other intangibles, 13 out of 15 of participants (87%) stated they used formal project management tools like Microsoft Project. However, seven out of 15 participants (47%) felt the tools were too complicated to use. Eight of 15 participants (53%) stated the project managers had a difficult time using the project management tools effectively. Participants said that keeping good risks and issues log, regular status reporting, change management, proper testing with no short-cuts, and setting a defined closure date were good practices that they wished project managers would incorporate into their projects. Participants stated that accepting bad test results, not delivering on requirements, lack of communications, and not managing to stakeholders led to failures.

Many factors can lead a project to failure; however, with identifications of flawed areas, recommendations can be made to mitigate unfortunate events. There was no phase of the project life cycle that was immune to problems and conflicts. A project could fail at any point in time, so recommendations must cover each phase of the project life cycle.

As for the project managers, participants said projects failed because the project managers lacked experience or training. Participants found that both set of expectations were necessary. A project manager with many years of experience with little formal education struggled to keep the project running smoothly. On the other extreme side, a project manager that took many classes and seminars on project management but had little experience had difficulty keeping momentum on the project. Participants stated the best chance for success is an experience project manager with formal training or certifications in project management leading the project.

Like most situations, intelligence combined with formal education can increase individuals' chance for project success. Applying the University of Phoenix's Scholar, Practitioner, Leadership Model (SPL), a project manager who implemented project management activities (practitioner) must be formally educated in the art of project management (scholar) to lead a project to success (leadership). This researcher thought that there was tremendous value in project management education and certification to build a strong foundation for a project manager to lead the delivery of a project to success.

Figure 7 contained data that aided in the development of the themes and sub-themes. Categories that had a high percentage of participants' claiming areas of project failures led the researcher to review specific sections of participants' interviews. Despite this researcher interviewing different participants about their experience at different companies, the problem areas leading to project failure were consistent throughout the study. This researcher discovered several project management best practices from the participants' interviews that were helpful in drawing conclusions and developing the recommendations.

Themes and Sub-themes	Participant 001	002	003	004	005	006	007	008	009	010	011	012	013	014	015	n	%
1) Problems in Requirements Phase	x	x	x	x	x	x	x	x	x	x	x	x	x	x	x	15	100%
Review of requirements	x	x	x	x	x	x										6	40%
Planning to meet requirements	x	x	x	x	x	x	x	x	x	x	x	x	x	x	x	15	100%
Setup the project	x	x		x			x		x		x	x		x		8	53%
Initiate the project	x	x		x			x		x		x		x		x	8	53%
2) Problems in Development Phase	x	x	x	x	x	x	x	x	x	x	x		x	x	x	14	93%
Lack of communications between team members		x	x	x					x	x	x	x		x	x	9	60%
No idea of progress		x		x		x			x							4	27%
Development work did not match back to requirements	x			x	x	x		x			x	x	x	x	x	10	67%
3) Problems in Testing Phase	x	x		x	x	x	x	x	x	x	x	x	x	x	x	14	93%
Review of test results	x	x	x		x	x		x		x	x	x	x	x		11	73%
Audit of test cases	x	x	x	x	x		x	x		x	x	x	x		x	12	80%
Conflict of interest	x	x	x	x	x	x	x	x		x	x	x	x	x		13	87%
4) Problems in Deployment/Implementation Phase	x	x	x	x	x	x	x	x	x	x	x	x	x	x	x	15	100%
Customers not ready to accept project	x			x	x		x			x			x			6	40%
Testing was not sufficient	x	x		x			x	x	x	x	x	x	x	x	x	13	87%
5) Project Management tools	x	x	x	x	x	x	x			x	x	x	x	x	x	13	87%
Tools too complicated		x			x		x		x		x		x		x	7	47%
Project managers did not know how to use tools		x		x		x		x		x	x		x	x		8	53%
6) Leadership characteristics of Project Leaders	x	x	x	x	x	x	x	x	x	x	x	x	x	x	x	15	100%
Lazy		x				x							x			3	20%
Lack of experience	x					x			x	x	x					5	33%
Not flexible	x	x									x	x	x	x		6	40%
Not people friendly	x			x			x	x	x	x						6	40%
Poor communicator	x	x			x	x		x	x		x	x			x	9	60%
7) Best Practices in Project Management	x	x	x	x	x	x	x	x	x	x	x	x	x	x	x	15	100%
Kept risks and issues log	x			x	x	x	x	x	x	x	x	x	x	x	x	13	87%
Weekly or daily status reporting	x			x	x		x		x		x	x	x	x		9	60%
Follow change management process	x	x	x	x				x	x	x	x	x	x	x	x	12	80%
Plan and implement testing without taking shortcuts				x	x	x	x	x	x	x			x	x	x	10	67%
Set a closure date		x		x	x	x	x	x	x	x	x	x	x	x	x	13	87%
8) Worst Practices in Project Management	x	x	x	x	x	x	x	x	x	x	x	x	x	x	x	15	100%
Accepted bad test results					x			x	x	x	x	x	x	x	x	9	60%
Did not deliver on requirements					x	x				x	x	x				5	33%
No communications	x	x	x		x	x			x	x	x					8	53%
Did not manage up to stake holders	x		x		x					x	x					5	33%
9) Experience Levels of Project Managers	x	x	x	x	x	x	x	x	x	x	x	x	x	x	x	15	100%
More experience project managers were more capable of navigating through issues	x	x	x	x	x	x	x	x	x	x	x	x	x	x	x	15	100%
10) Certifications of Project Managers	x	x	x		x	x	x	x	x	x	x	x	x	x	x	14	93%
Highly trained project managers were able to rely on training to get project out of trouble	x	x			x	x	x	x	x	x	x	x	x	x	x	13	87%

Figure 7: Summary Data of the 15 Participants' Answers to Research Questions

Summary

Chapter 4 contained the explanations and results of the interviews completed over the summer of 2012 on 15 participants in the Research Triangle Park, North Carolina area with experience in failed IT projects in the pharmaceutical industry. Chapter 4 contained visual presentation of the data collection using nVivo10 software. This researcher used nVivo 10 to pinpoint the themes and sub-themes that emerged in this study. The demographic information of the 15 participants was split into three groups: (a) stakeholders, (b) project managers, and (c) project team members.

From the data analysis, researcher detected 10 emerging themes and 30 sub-themes of reasons why projects failed. The key themes were (1) failure during requirements phase (4 sub-themes), (2) failure during development phase (3 sub-themes), (3) failure during testing phase (3 sub-themes), (4) failure during deployment and implementation phase (2 sub-themes), (5) complication of project management tools (2 sub-themes), (6) leadership characteristics of project managers on failed project (5 sub-themes), (7) best practices in project management (5 sub-themes), (8) worst practices in project management (4 sub-themes), (9) experience level of project managers (1 sub-theme), and (10) education and certification level of project managers (1 sub-theme). Chapter 5 contained the IPA interpretations on the data analysis, conclusions, and recommendations for this study.

Chapter 5: Conclusions and Recommendations

The general problem addressed in this current qualitative phenomenological study was the high failure rate of IT projects in pharmaceutical industry (PMI, 2009). The specific problem addressed was the lack of understanding about the reasons why the continued high rate of IT projects failures (Cerpa & Verner, 2009). The study involved examination of leadership models and theories. Leadership models and theories included (a) Frederick Taylor's scientific management theory, (b) Vroom-Yetton Jago decision model, (c) Rogers' diffusion of innovation theory, (d) Henri Fayol's management theory, and (e) Douglas McGregor's Theory X and Y (Weiyin, Thong, Chasalow, & Dhillon, 2011).

Data collection involved in-person and over-the-phone interviews with15 stakeholders, project managers, and project team members who had first-hand experience in failed IT projects in pharmaceutical industry located in or conducting business in Research Triangle Park, North Carolina. A failed IT project was a project that did not complete on time, within budget, or with quality. Stakeholders, project managers, and project team members included vice presidents, various directors of information technology departments, project managers, developers, testers, programmers, and analysts.

As discussed in Chapter 4, researcher discovered 10 themes and 30 sub-themes originated from the data analysis of the 15 participants' answers. After careful evaluation and interpretation of the 10 themes and 30 sub-themes, this researcher made six conclusions and provided recommendations to mitigate the conclusions.

Ethical Dimensions

The researcher approached this research study with high ethical standards and followed the rules of the Protection of Human Research Participants throughout the research process, especially during the data collection process. Researcher paid special attentions to privacy protection during interviews by informing participants of confidentiality expectations and receiving signatures before interviews.

Researcher entered each interview with a clear and open mind. Researcher handled the interviews with honesty and high regard for professionalism. Handwritten interview data was locked away in a combination briefcase, and electronic data was kept in a password protected laptop to ensure confidentiality. Pseudonym designations aided in maintaining privacy, and the researcher did not share their names with anyone.

Limitations

Limitations were challenges or flaws to the study (Neuman, 2006). This study contained limitations combined with (a) location of participants, (b) participant cooperation level, and (c) over-generalization. The participants in this research study were from the geography of Research Triangle Park, North Carolina. The limiting factor was the study's data was representation of Research Triangle Park only and did not include reasoning why IT projects failed in other geographies.

Another limitation was the small participant sample size of 15 to explore why IT projects failed. The participants were selected from surveys collected at the local PMI chapter in Research Triangle Park, North Carolina. The answers in the surveys identified the industries they work in, level of experience in project management, and roles in the projects. The participants were stakeholders, project managers, and project team members who participated with IT projects in the pharmaceutical industry. The stakeholders provided details on when and why they thought the projects started failing. The project managers offered details on the initial categories of the project management process. Project team members provided yet another level of details because they were intimate to certain phases of the project management processes. Combined, these participants produced insight to the IT projects failure phenomenon. The findings were from Research Triangle Park IT projects, but may lead to over-generalization that IT projects outside of this geographic area will have the same findings. To address the overgeneralization potential, the study included specific factors from the details of the interviews on the phenomenon of why IT projects failed in the pharmaceutical industry (Neuman, 2006).

Conclusions Overview

The purpose of this study was to answer the research question: why do IT projects continue to fail at a high rate in the pharmaceutical industry? Chapter 4 above contained data analysis to answer the research question, and there were several interpretations and conclusions. The interpretation of findings led to the emergence of six key conclusions from the interviews with 15 participants in this qualitative phenomenological study presented here in Chapter 5.

Conclusion 1: Project Failed Because of Poor Requirements

During data analysis, 15 out of 15 participants (100%) stated they had problems in requirements phase. Problems ranged from not planning for the requirements, and lack of initiations between groups. For example, the customers thought that the project leaders would ask for clarification if needed, but nobody did. The project manager and project team thought that they would receive more information from the customers and patiently waited while precious project time was wasted. Interpretation was that the various parties did not understand what they were asking for and what the developers would eventually design. The first conclusion was poor requirements led to project failure.

Conclusion 2: Project Failed Because Risks and Issues Not Managed

At a higher level, this conclusion was a communication breakdown between stakeholders, project managers, and project team members. However, communication was a broad category and further analysis required. A deeper analysis led this researcher to discover the underlying problem was that the project manager did not communicate risks and issues properly to concerning parties. Project managers failed to communicate because they did not manage risks and issues well enough to understand themselves what to communicate. The conclusion was lack of proper management of risks and issues led to project failure.

Conclusion 3: Project Failed Because No Management of Scope Change

In data analysis, 10 out of 15 participants (67%) stated that changes in scope confused the project teams. The interpretation after reviewing several participants' answers was that the requirements kept changing; so therefore, scope changed too. Customers had the right to change their minds about scope, but the project manager failed to adjust the project plan by following proper change control. For example, customer originally wanted 10 application servers, and then they wanted 12 application servers after the project started. Project manager agreed to the change but did not modify schedule, budget, or resources to take on extra work. Interpretation was managing scope change was lacking, and conclusion was this short coming led to project failure.

Conclusion 4: Project Failed Because of Poor Project Leadership

In reviewing the data, 14 of 15 participants (93%) stated the project manager could improve on formal project management. Project management basics such as communication, planning, status tracking, and status meetings were not used throughout the project. The project managers were not trained or lacked experience in the art of project management. Some were appointed the project management positions because of their strong background in technical skills. The interpretation was missing project management fundamentals led to many challenges on the project. The conclusion was poor project management led to failed projects.

Conclusion 5: Project Failed Because of Improper Testing

After careful review, 12 out of 15 participants (80%) that projects failed during testing phase. Participants cited poor test cases, testing, and a rushed schedule for failure in testing phase. A deeper analysis led to an interpretation of a conflict of interest between testers and project manager. Because the test manager and tester reported to the project manager in an organizational hierarchy, the project manager could influence the test results. A conclusion was problems in testing phase led to project failure.

Conclusion 6: Project Failed Because It Was Kept Open Indefinitely

In reviewing the data, researcher discovered 13 out of 15 participants (87%) stated that the projects went on too long. An interpretation was no one really set a closure date because a project team was already in place, and stakeholders and customers did not want to start another project. Instead of going through the hassle of starting a new project, customers just added more work to an existing project and eventually the project team reached a breaking point because of exhaustion. The interpretation was that project was intentionally kept open, and a conclusion was not having project closure management led to project failure.

Best Leadership Theory for Project Management

Based on the results, this researcher concluded Henri Fayol's management theory was most beneficial to the project management life cycle (Pryor & Taneja, 2010). Henri Fayol was known as the father of modern operational management theory (Pryor & Taneja, 2010). Fayol's theory contrasted from Frederick Taylor's theory because Fayol looked at management from the executive view, but Taylor focused on the individual worker skill levels (McLean, 2011). However, this current study can benefit from having a top-down and bottom-up analysis of pharmaceutical project management. Fayol identified five primary objectives for management as (a) planning, (b) managing, (c) commanding, (d) facilitating, and (e) controlling (McLean, 2011). To supplement these objectives, Fayol also explained the 14 principles of management listed below (Pryor & Taneja, 2010):

1. Specialization of labor: project team members continued to improve their skills.
2. Authority: project managers had the right to command.
3. Discipline: project leader can discipline when orders were not followed.
4. Unity of command: Each project had one project manager/leader.
5. Unity of direction: Each project followed one project plan.
6. Subordination of individual interests: Project team members primarily discussed project activities not personal agendas
7. Remuneration: Stakeholders, project managers, and project team members were financially compensated fairly.
8. Centralization: Executives provided the leadership and direction for the team.
9. Chain of Superiors: Each employee had a supervisor.
10. Order: Employees had a place for work such as offices or cubicles assigned to them.
11. Equity: Employees expected and received fair treatment (no harassment).
12. Personnel Tenure: Management should try to keep good employees happy, so they stayed longer with the company.
13. Initiative: Planned and implemented (do not just talk about; do it).
14. Esprit de corps: Management should strive for harmony on project teams.

Suggestions for Future Research

This researcher suggested further investigation if the below six recommendations were implemented at pharmaceutical companies and to study their success improvement rates. Researcher recommended if future studies could be conducted outside of the Research Triangle Park, North Carolina region to determine effectiveness of the recommendations. Researcher recommended a large sample size, and maybe exploring a study to see if project performance did improve with using these recommendations.

This researcher suggested conducting future separate qualitative studies for each recommendation to really understand what can be done for continuous improvements. The six recommendations represented a high-level interpretation of what the participants thought caused projects to fail. However, breaking up the recommendations into distinct future research studies may permit formation of better mitigation plans to prevent project failure.

Another suggestion for future research was to explore the effectiveness and practicality of Henri Fayol's management theory in an organization's project management activities. The 14 steps of Henri Fayol's management theory can be used as research questions for future studies. Furthermore, future researchers can explore in details each of the 14 steps to discover if Henri Fayol's management theory was still viable in today's project management culture.

Recommendations Overview

The recommendations were relevant to companies in the pharmaceutical industry, and the results of this study provided the stakeholders, project managers, and project team members a clear understanding of why projects failed and what changes can be made to increase chances of success. This study contained analysis of the key project life-cycle phases and details on what went wrong in each phase from different perspectives of stakeholders, project managers, and project team members.

These recommendations may aid future project leaders in improving project success records of the IT components in drug development projects by better understanding what went wrong and how a diverse group of participants would have addressed the projects in hindsight. Drugs can save lives and bringing drugs to market faster was an imperative mission. The recommendations converged only on critical points to increase the level of success for IT projects in pharmaceutical industry. The recommendations aimed to address gaps in differences between successful projects and failed projects. Below were the recommendations that future stakeholders, project managers, and project team members should consider to successfully deliver projects on schedule, within budget, and with quality. The recommendations to increase the chance of projects success were to implement: (a) requirements management, (b) risks & issues management, (c) change management, (d) implementation management, (e) testing management, and (f) closure management. Figure 8 below listed the recommendations in a butterfly design on how to run a successful project.

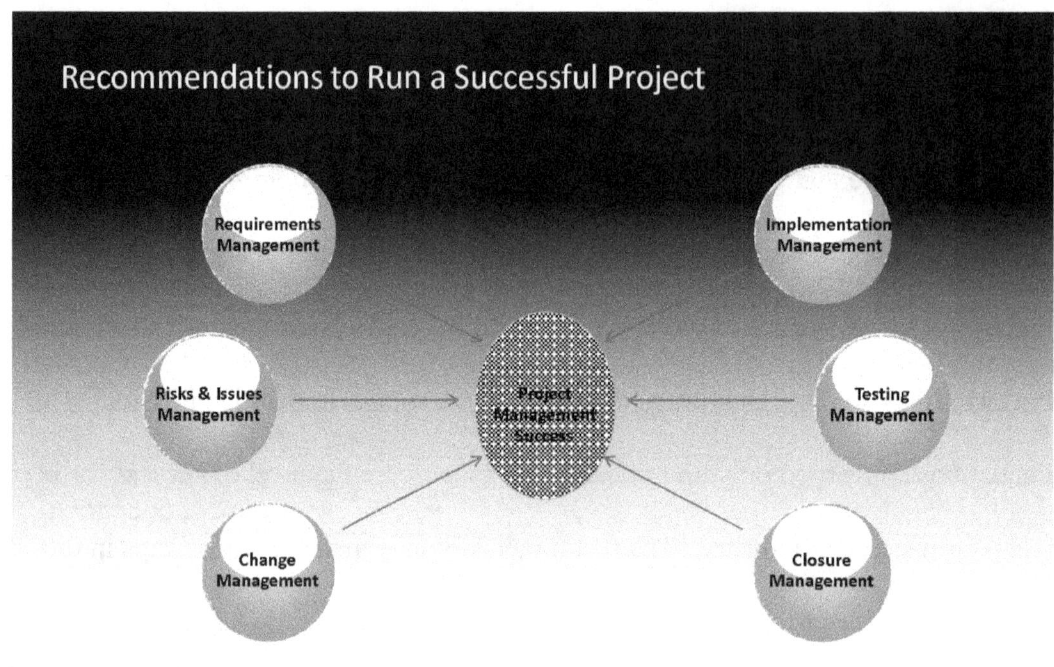

Figure 8: Six Recommendations for Project Success

Recommendation 1: Requirements Management

The project leaders needed to manage the customer's requirements by analyzing needs, constraints, and interfaces with other IT systems throughout the project. Stakeholders, project managers, and team members must understand business and user requirements and converted into technically implementable system requirements. During project planning, the related work products, plans, and activities must trace back to the requirements. Project leaders should review the requirements throughout the project life cycle from start to finish. Any changes to the requirements should follow a change management plan, which was part of another recommendation.

The main goals of requirements management were to generate clear, unambiguous requirements for approval by stakeholders and for application developers to understand the requirements. Furthermore, project managers must manage inconsistencies in the project plan in relations to requirements. Activities in the project plan must trace back to the requirements, otherwise a project manager must ask what the purpose was for that particular task. The requirements management process began when a request was made for an IT project. The project manager reviewed the requirements and documentation provided in support of the project. This knowledge transfer activity was to confirm scope and expectations of project delivery. Project managers and team members identified any inconsistencies during planning phase and clarified as needed during team meetings with the authors of the requirements to prevent second hand information.

After clarification of requirements, the project manager discussed requirements with other groups. Project manager and project team members elaborated on the requirements to determine if there were still ambiguity concerns, discussed operational scenarios, mapped for traceability, and correlated requirements with traceability. Furthermore, project manager confirmed interpretation back to customers for accuracy. Project manager discussed with IT architecture representatives if systems were feasible to implement requirements.

Once requirements were clarified, project manager communicated to stakeholders, project team members, and customers that requirements assessment was about to begin. This communication permitted stakeholders and customers one more opportunity to change minds before full approval work to begin. Project manager created a requirements traceability matrix mapping the expectations of the project back to requirements. The requirements traceability matrix must be updated regularly for proper status reporting. Any changes to requirements must follow the change management process. Documentation was archived on the company networks, so other employees can download for review. Project manager led the auditing of hardware, software, and other IT infrastructure components to collect inventory of existing systems. The project manager prepared a comprehensive list of inventory related to delivering on the requirements. Project manager added inventory components to a virtual library for coding and record keeping.

The purpose of collecting inventory components was for project manager to understand gaps between existing infrastructure items versus requirements expectations. Configuration of hardware and software items may change to accommodate requirements. Before modification of existing items, project manager led impact analysis of what modifications had on requirements. The project manager developed requirements checks to see if project need new infrastructure. For example, the requirements stated needing 15 database servers, but during inventory check, project team members discovered only 10 database servers. The gaps between inventory and requirements were documented and presented to stakeholders, so they can consider funding options.

The project manager created a requirements governance model to ensure compliance with external regulations such as US Department of Food & Drug Administration (FDA). Stakeholders, project managers, and project team members clearly tagged which requirements were driven by compliance because they were top priorities. Modification to existing systems must not break any compliance expectations. Governance permitted project manager to confirm quality and completeness of requirements. The boundaries of the requirements were clearly defined. Project manager provided sufficient coverage of the requirements, and understood nature of operational usage for each requirement. This due diligence permitted understanding interdependencies and interfaces between the requirements.

After compliance audit of the requirements, the project manager led the prioritizing of the requirements. This prioritizing permitted understanding which requirements provided essential business operation functionality. Consideration for prioritization included mandatory requirements, regulatory requirements and systems specific. The project manager considered constraints to the requirements from a safety, security, regulatory, technical, and operational perspectives. Project manager also considered assumptions about the requirements on systems development. Furthermore, project manager created list of risks about the requirements, and how each requirement depends on another requirement. Project manager must satisfy regulation standards.

After prioritizing of requirements, the project manager consulted with project team members to understand the usability of the requirements. Usability review aided in awareness of how the users will receive the requirements. This usability reviewer should have a vested interest in the outcome of the project. Projects without usability review were subject to challenges during integration.

The requirements management phase ended with approved, archived requirements documentations and creation of a requirement traceability matrix. Project programmers and system developers reviewed the requirements for comprehension. Purpose of review was to understand the scope of systems and environment requirements, the priorities, infrastructure consideration, operational functions, usability, and external compliance factors.

Recommendation 2: Risks and Issues Management

A risk was an event that had a chance of occurring on the project (PMI, 2008). When a risk matured, it became an issue that needed mitigation (PMI, 2008). For example, there was a risk that our application server could get infected with a computer virus. When the application server was infected, the risk became an issue that required immediate resolution.

Risk Management

Risk management was the process to identify, analyze, monitor, and mitigate risks associated in an IT project (PMI, 2008). Risk management permitted a project manager to highlight risks to stakeholders in advance of risks maturing into potential issues. Avoiding or mitigating the risk aided increasing change of project success.

First, the project manager identified risks by filling out risk identification checklist using project approved risk guidelines. The project manager identified the risks with assistance from the project team members and key stakeholders. Project manager included risks for tracking in the risk tracker. Project manager used the risk identification checklist as a trigger to identify potential risks that threaten the delivery of the project on time, within budget, and with quality. The project manager clearly defined the risks in the project risk tracker with statements explaining the risks. The risk tracker list grew as the project progressed. Project manager studied potential failure modes, and the project manager followed up with a risk impact and probability matrix. These assessments permitted a project manager to quantify the risks for cost/effort, schedule, and performance of project. Project manager identified risks as high, medium, or low with probability also as high, medium, or low. Project manager provided this information in the risk management tracker. Risk mitigation and contingency planning began with high impact, high probability risks and finished with low impact, low probability risks.

There were two types of plans to address risks. A contingency plan was an action that should be taken when a risk matures. A mitigation plan was when action taken to minimize risk from maturing into an issue. The project manager actively reviewed and updated the risk tracker. If a risk occurred, project manager activated either contingency or mitigation plan based on agreed steps in risk tracker. Early on the project, there were not many risks, but as project continued, new risks were added as more information was made available. The project manager should monitor and track open risks to closure. Poor risk management was a leading cause of project failure during data analysis of the participants' interviews. Project manager communicated risk management to stakeholders to seek guidance on risks that jeopardized a project delivery. Project manager added risk log to status reporting with category ranking and action items listed. Risk management continued through the life-cycle of the project.

Issues Management

Issues management process included the tracking, controlling, and resolution of issues that rose during the project (PMI, 2008). Project manager developed an issue management plan in parallel with the project plan. Stakeholders approved the issues management plan because of potential bearing to project budget. Most issues were risks from the risk tracker, so stakeholders knew them in advance.

Project manager identified an issue owner to see through resolution of issue. An issue owner was someone who had strong technical knowledge of the issue. The issue owner categorized the issue as high, medium, or low based on agreed guidelines. Issue owner quantified number of days delay in a project, if any. If resolution required a change to project scope, the project manager followed the change management process. Project manager worked with issue owner till resolution of issue.

Recommendation 3: Change Management

The purpose of change management was to define a management process to request changes to a project. The objectives of change were to (a) provide a mechanism to track and control changes, (b) ensure that only approved changes will be undertaken and deployed, (c) permit stakeholders to make decisions in an open and timely manner, (d) assist in keeping project scope, timelines, and budget within range, and (e) maintain traceability throughout the project life cycle. Categories of changes included change in requirements, resources, schedule, or budget.

Requests for changes to a project may come from stakeholders, project manager, project team members, or customers. The status of each change request was recorded in a change log, which contained information on all changes. Table 10 below contained coding for change status.

Table 10

Description of Change Status

Status	**Description**
Approved	Stakeholders approved the request.
Assessed	The assessment was documented. Awaiting approval to accept and progress the request.
Closed – Cancelled	The Change Request was withdrawn and not implemented.
Closed – Deferred	Change Request closed due to delay, postponement or overdue.
Closed – Deployed	Impacted project items had been updated.
Closed – Rejected	Stakeholders did not approve the request following the assessment.
Deferred	If the Change Request was delayed, postponed or overdue.

New	A new request that was ready for assessment and consideration.
Verified	The Changes were completed.
Revisit	The Change Request had not met the exit criteria.

First step, the need for a change was identified. Project manager entered a change request into the change log. Project manager requested contributions from stakeholders and project team members. Based on justification, project manager evaluated the change and solicited consultation from a subject matter expert if change should be implemented at current phase of project.

Second, the project team members conducted technical assessment of the change request, indentifying any dependent items, which may also require change. The assessment involved the project team members, and the project manager assigned or delegated the task of assessment and estimation to others outside of the team. The purpose of technical assessment was to determine impact of the change on the project. Project manager reviewed relevant project items and documentation should be referenced during the analysis activity. Project manager documented the assessment and ensured that there was enough information to implement the change request. Project manager identified which phase of the project for execution of the change. Project manager followed best practices similar to work breakdown structure (WBS), function point, or Delphi technique. Project manager included personnel assessment as well.

Once completion of justification and determination due diligence, project manager brought the change request to the stakeholders for review with recommendation to approve or reject the change. Based on the recommendation to approve or reject, the stakeholders voted to concur or over-rule. In either case, hand-written signature was required for archiving. Rejected change must be sign-off to incase of future questions.

If stakeholders approved change request, project manager planned for and implemented the change. Project manager added new tasks to project plan, and logged additional training modules for users and customers to learn about the change. Implementation of the change ended the change management process.

Recommendation 4: Project Implementation Management

The purpose of project implementation management was to define the execution parameters of IT projects. Project implementation management contained processes to cover kick-off, planning, monitoring, and controlling of projects. Project implementation management contained best practices and guidelines for delivery of the project. Project implementation phase cannot start until after requirements sign-off.

First, project manager reviewed the requirements, scope, and resources available for the project. Project manager reviewed goals, deliverables, team composition, and technologies availability. Project manager developed the life cycle model of activities, work products, and reviews for the project and wrote the information in the project plan. It was possible that requirements changed from preparation stage, and project manager confirmed accuracy of requirements. Project manager checked for completion of the following key activities:

1. Project requirements were adequately documented for managing the project.
2. Detailed estimates and schedules of quality planning parameters were established and maintained.
3. Project activities were identified, established and maintained in the quality plan including references to the change management process.

4. Resource planning and resource Identification setup.
5. Completion of start-up formalities and physical office environment set up.
6. Provided access permissions to project resources.
7. Identified and conducted the required trainings.
8. Reviewed and confirmed the project life cycle model.
9. Created a project plan for tracking.
10. Identified the project risks and issues and added to log.
11. Identified the work allocation of project team members.

Next, project manager identified the resource requirements in consultation with stakeholders. Results of consultation included (a) skills required, (b) schedule of the project, (c) experience of the team members, and (d) contact information of resources. Other considerations included travel schedule and different time zone working hours.

Then project manager inducted the resources by asking the new project team members to review requirements and expectations of the project. For quality control, team members signed off on their understanding of the requirements. After confirmation of understanding the requirements, project manager arranged for access permission to hardware, software, and network for team members. Team members completed appropriate training for hardware, software, and network security features for record keeping. Project manager started adding team members to the project plan and sent documentation to team members for review. Project manager reviewed and confirmed project plan and work expectations with team members.

Project manager scheduled a project kick-off meeting with stakeholders and project team members to highlight (a) project scope and objectives, (b) roles and responsibilities, (c) key milestones and deliverables, and (d) project management approach. Project manager reminded the team on current risks and issues for monitoring. Even though their services were not required yet, project manager invited testers to the kick-off meeting for their understanding and expectations.

After project work started, project manager needed to monitor and control project implementation. Project manager identified the key measures to review for the project by indicating purpose for each measure. Project manager tracked the schedule, budget, and efforts measures at least once a week to ensure that efforts, tasks completion, and communications were constant. This monitoring aided project manager in seeing potential deviations early on the project. Project manager monitored risks and issues logs for potential surprises. Project manager sent status reporting once a week to the stakeholders and highlighting planned versus actual variance on cost, schedule, and efforts.

Project manager conducted weekly status review meetings to discuss progress of the project. At the minimum, agenda topics were (a) progress, (b) risks and issues, (c) schedule, and (d) any change request. Project manager discussed the important aspects of project execution including resourcing and development progress. Project manager requested support from stakeholders for escalations. Project implementation phase ended with approval and confirmation of successful test results.

Recommendation 5: Testing and Inspection Management

Testing and inspection management were critical to ensuring quality of deliverables by showing repeatability and predictability of project implementation. Testing confirmed delivery of requirements and compliance across internal and external standards such as Food & Drug

Administration (FDA). Stakeholders, project manager, and project team members developed and reviewed testing plan together.

Testing began after completion of development work in project implementation phase. Project manager notified test manager and testing team that deliverables were ready for formal testing. The test manager was responsible for filling out testing documentation with results. For example, testing manager noted what testing procedures were used and in what areas of the project. Test manager included reference to (a) test procedures, (b) test templates, (c) testing checklist, and (d) reviews of testers.

Testers noted use of testing best practices, lapses in test results, and classification of lapses. Testers classified failed components as critical, major, minor, or alerting only. Testers notified test manager a corrective action plan with recommendations on owner and completion date. A test result document included the following:

- Test Title - Used standard operating procedure or relevant test documents to describe the subject matter.
- Test Description - A brief factual description of the test deficiency, the project phase or the area affected.
- Testing Supporting Evidence - This should be either a numbered, lettered or bulleted list of observations supporting the finding, whichever format was used should be used consistently throughout the report. The facts should be reported as observed with attachment of evidence via a screen shot of success confirmation.

Table 11 contained information on the classification for testing. Different criticality levels required different mitigation plans. The descriptions with information permitted test managers or testers to make informed decisions.

Table 11

Description of Testing Classification

Test Classification	Description of Test Classification
Critical	Required that further operations stop until corrective action was completed.
Major	Required an immediate corrective action plan and response although operations can proceed.
Minor	Required corrective action, minor observations were those that deviated from accepted standards but had a relatively low probability of affecting the quality.
Note	A deficiency, bud did not warrant attention.

Conflict of Interest Resolution

During data analysis, 14 of 15 (93%) participants felt project managers did or were in position to manipulate test results. This researcher proposed a change to the reporting structure of a typical project where the tester reported to the stakeholders and not the project manager. This change in reporting structure mitigated a conflict of interest. Figure 9 showed a current, typical organization, and Figure 10 contained a recommended organization chart change.

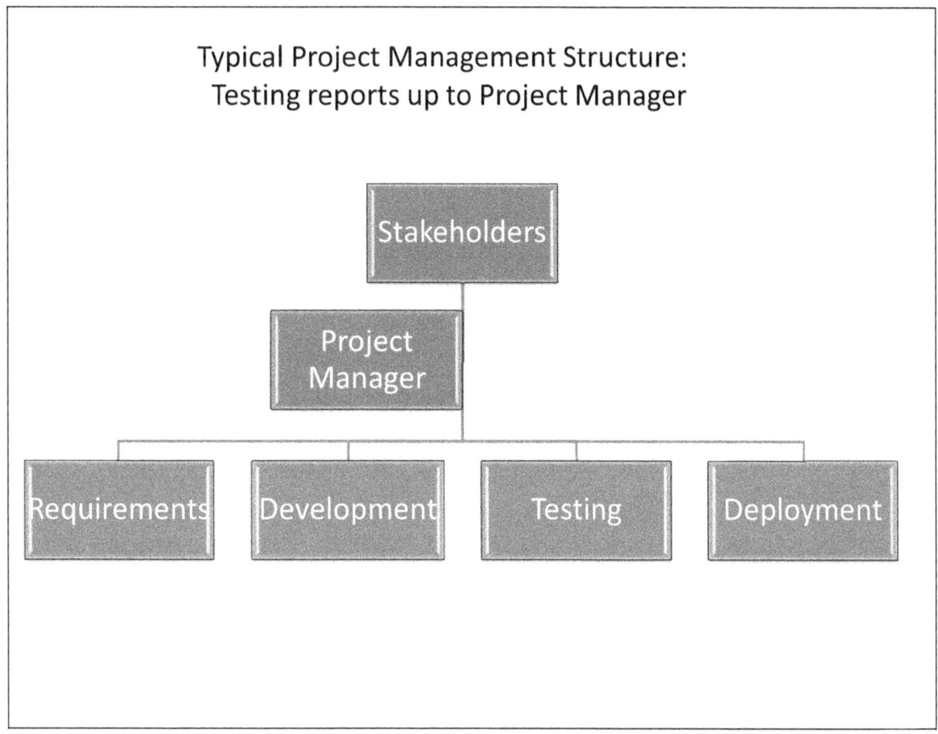

Figure 9: Current and Typical Reporting Structure

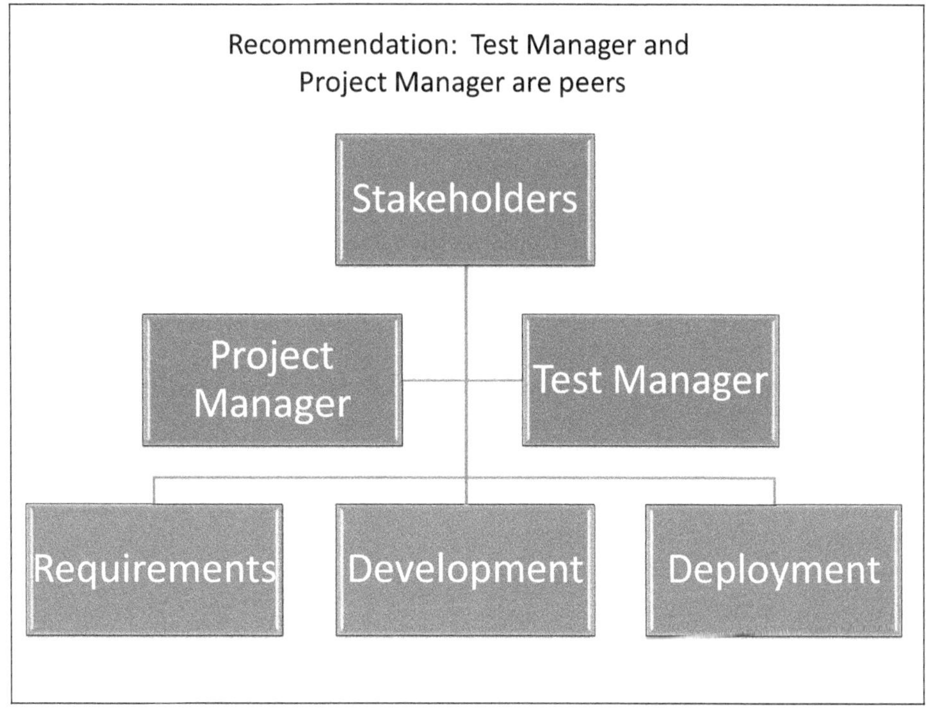

Figure 10: Recommended Organization Reporting Structure

In Figure 10, to eliminate conflict of interest, test manager should not report to project manager. Test manager instructed testers to complete repeated iterations of testing until defects were addressed. Testing phase ended with approval of testing results by stakeholders. Project manager can provide input, but to eliminate conflict of interest, stakeholders were final approvers.

Recommendation 6: Closure Management

The purpose of project closure management was to ensure systematic closure of a project and shared the best practices that worked and lessons learned. Project manager checked to see if deliverables completed and requirements fulfilled. Project manager ensured closure of items in change requests and risks and issues logs. Project manager provided a closure meeting and discussed lessons learned. Furthermore, project manager requested revoking access to production systems. Project manager confirmed closure of requirements and deliverables by archiving signatures sign-off. Project manager checked to see if the deliverables fulfilled the requirements, and deliverables transitioned to support. Project manager provided a list of training modules for customers and users to attend.

The project manager performed a retrospective analysis with stakeholders and project team members after signatures sign-off to close project. Project manager reviewed metrics data and other project performance measures to see which activities were challenging to the project team members. Project manager performed lessons learned with team members to discuss:

1. Root cause analysis of problems
2. What best practices worked
3. Process improvements for future projects
4. Reuse of hardware or software

5. Documentation storage
6. Final review of cost, schedule, and quality

Project manager prepared a project closure report and stating where important project documentations were archived. In the closure report, project manager listed future project and process improvement recommendations. Just as important, project manager initiated decommission of computer, software, and network infrastructure. Project manager revoked access permissions for project team members. During interviews of participants, some past project team members still had access to systems and accidentally corrupted important system files.

Significant to Leadership

The high failure rate of IT projects in drug development companies in the pharmaceutical industry was alarming. Drugs were literally a matter of life or death to for patients with critical health ailments. The six recommendations of proper management listed above contained potentially successful leadership strategies to improve project success rate. The recommendations should be helpful to organizational leaders of pharmaceutical companies to achieve better success in project management.

As a potential important collateral benefit of this research study, organizational leaders could use the six recommendations to save money because projects cost over-run could be substantial and devastating to some companies. With the US economy slowly recovering from a recession at the time of writing on this research paper, organizational leaders were still closely watching expenditures at companies operating in the US. The point was having a better grasp on project management could save money and boost hiring and bring more jobs.

Significant to Academic Leadership

From an academic standpoint, this researcher contributed project management research specific to pharmaceutical companies to academic and sociological literature. Project management best practices, project manager's roles and responsibilities, leadership and management styles, and project strategies could help organizational leaders achieve better success. To achieve business objectives, leaders implemented projects, and having proper project management skills could be beneficial in achieving success.

The results and recommendations of this study were significant to both scholars and practitioners. Scholars received a new project management body of knowledge framework from this paper. Project Management Institute (PMI) scholars could review their current project life cycle and may make modifications. Furthermore, PMI scholars may create new pharmaceutical project management best practices. Practitioners could avoid many mistakes highlighted in this study, and they should have preventative measures in place as discussed in this paper.

Reflections

Drugs were critical to patients' safety and health. In this century's high tech society, drug development projects depended on IT components for successful market launch. Understanding why the IT projects continually failed and development of recommendations to mitigate project failures made this researcher excited. This researcher was grateful for the opportunities to interview passionate people in pharmaceutical companies from diverse backgrounds and different IT areas. The researcher was proud of the efforts gave by caring people and sacrifices they made for drug development.

During residency in the early days of this researcher's doctorate journey, a professor challenged the class members to pick a dissertation topic that was important and worthwhile to each of them. The researcher picked this topic because of the potential life savings recommendations and was proud to develop this study. Almost anyone reading this research study will most likely know of someone who was better today because of life-saving drugs that came to market just in time.

Summary

The general problem addressed in this current study was the analysis and explanation of the high failure rate of IT projects in pharmaceutical industry. The failure rate of IT projects was greater than 72% (PMI, 2009). In 2007, the Standish Group reported IT projects success rate were only at 35% (Cerpa & Verner, 2009). In 2011, project success was up slightly to 37% ("Failure rates finally drop," 2011). The high failure rate delayed drug development. People were dependent on drugs to cure troublesome diseases and other ailments. Some people even depended on drugs to save their lives or the lives of loved ones. Drug development was not fast enough because many factors lead to delays in launching new drug products (Kaitin, 2010). A delay in drug launch set back a company on average $15 million per day on each drug (Noffke, 2007). Drug launch delay (a) diminished a company to earn back research and development cost, (b) left door open for competition to release their versions of similar drugs, and (c) left patients waiting for a safe treatment options (Noffke, 2007). One critical factor was the IT projects that supported drug development were constantly taking longer than expected (Civan & Maloney, 2009).

The specific problem was the lack of comprehension about the reasons that IT projects failed at such a high rate. A report by PMI stated poor project management and implementation skills were two key factors in project failures (PMI, 2009). Failures in information technology projects delayed the delivery of drugs to patients which needed the drugs to get better and live longer (PMI, 2009). The problem was that information technology projects in pharmaceutical companies continue to fail because of (a) finishing late, (b) over-budget, or with (c) low quality causing delays in drug development to save people's lives. For example, Pfizer Pharmaceutical's Lipitor cholesterol drug delay would cost the company $35 million per day (Noffke, 2007). The latest report showed 42 million Americans suffered from high cholesterol, and this drug delay would limit their treatment choices (WebMD, 2012). Drug development cost on only one drug could be as high as $2 billion, so drug companies were eager to recoup drug research cost quickly (Mikhail & Giddings, 2011).

The current study represented a phenomenological research design within a qualitative research method. As the objective of this current study was to analyze the IT projects failures phenomenon through the first-hand experiences of project team members, stakeholders, and project managers who participated on the projects, a phenomenological research design was suitable for the current qualitative study. Qualitative was appropriate over quantitative for this study because the focus was to answer "why" projects are continuing to fail at a high rate (Leedy & Ormrod, 2010). IT projects were unique, had a clear start and end date, and added functionality to hardware, software, or network infrastructure (PMI, 2009). People planned, implemented, and controlled IT projects with focus on formal project management methodology (PMI, 2009). The general population of the current study was the project managers, team members, and stakeholders within the Research Triangle Park, North Carolina pharmaceutical companies. The stakeholders were in positions of authorities in dealing with the project management activities of the IT projects, such as Director of Projects, Director of ERP, and Vice President (VP) of IT.

The researcher conducted a qualitative phenomenological study from June 2012 to August 2012 to explore the perceptions of 15 IT personnel from pharmaceutical companies in Research Triangle Park in Raleigh, North Carolina who witnessed first-hand on what factors caused project failures. Phenomenological research had been a popular qualitative research strategy for the last 20 years (Shank, 2006). Phenomenological research was about the assumption that subjects of research had a conscious and can share valuable insight (Willis, 2007). Phenomenological research distinguished between noumena or real things and the perceptions of them or phenomena (Willis, 2007, p. 172). Therefore, phenomenological research focused on consciousness and perception (Neuman, 2006). The main task of phenomenological research was identifying common themes in people's descriptions of their own perceptions on how the projects failed (Leedy & Ormrod, 2010). Researchers obtained data for phenomenological research by interviewing and questioning participants (Willis, 2007). A researcher's goal was to understand the participant experience and perception of the situation (Leedy & Ormrod, 2010).

This researcher discovered 10 themes and 30 sub-themes originated from the data analysis of the 15 participants' answers. After careful evaluation and interpretation of the 10 themes and 30 sub-themes, this researcher made six conclusions and provided recommendations to address the conclusions. The recommendations were relevant to companies in the pharmaceutical industry, and the results of this study provided the stakeholders, project managers, and project team members a clear understanding of why projects failed and what changes can be made to increase chances of success. This study contained analysis of the key project life-cycle phases and details on what went wrong in each phase from different perspectives of stakeholders, project managers, and project team members.

These recommendations may aid future project leaders in improving project success records of the IT components in drug development projects by better understanding what went wrong and how a diverse group of participants would have addressed the projects in hindsight. Drugs can save lives and bringing drugs to market faster was an imperative mission. The recommendations converged only on critical points to increase the level of success for IT projects in pharmaceutical industry. The recommendations aimed to address gaps in differences between successful projects and failed IT projects in pharmaceutical industry. This researcher made recommendations that organizational leaders should consider to successfully deliver projects on schedule, within budget, and with quality. Thank you.

References

AbdelMalik, P., Boulos, M., & Jones, R. (2008). The perceived impact of location privacy: a web-based survey of public health perspectives and requirements in the UK and Canada. *BMC Public Health*, 8156-174.

Ahmad, N., & Alahakoon, D. (2010). Generating concept trees from dynamic self-organizing Map. *World Academy of Science, Engineering & Technology, 65,* 706-711.

Al-Ahmad, W., Al-Fagih, K., Khanfar, K., Alsamara, K., Abuleil, S., & Abu-Salem, H. (2009). A taxonomy of an IT project failure: root causes. *International Management Review, 5*(1), 93-104.

Alnaser, M. (2009). Psychosocial issues of work-related musculoskeletal injuries and adaptation: a phenomenological study. *Work, 32*(2), 123-132. doi:http://dx.doi.org.ezproxy.apollolibrary.com/10.3233/WOR-2009-0798

Appan, R., & Browne, G. J. (2010). Investigating retrieval-induced forgetting during information requirements determination. *Journal of the Association for Information Systems*, *11*(5), 250-275.

Arain, M., Campbell, M., Cooper, C., & Lancaster, G. (2010). What is a pilot or feasibility study? A review of current practice and editorial policy. *BMC Medical Research Methodology*, 1067.

Aramo-Immonen, H., & Vanharanta, H. (2009). Project management: The task of holistic systems thinking. *Human Factors & Ergonomics in Manufacturing, 19*(6), 582-600. doi:10.1002/hfm.

Athreye, S., & Godley, A. (2009). Internationalization and technological leapfrogging in the pharmaceutical industry. *Industrial & Corporate Change*, *18*(2), 295-323.

Bardhan, I. R., Krishnan, V. V., & Lin, S. (2007). Project performance and the enabling role of information technology: An exploratory study on the role of alignment. *Manufacturing & Service Operations Management, 9*(4), 579-595.

Benţa, D., Podean, I., & Mircean, C. (2011). On best practices for risk management in complex projects. *Informatica Economica, 15*(2), 142-152.

Besner, C., & Hobbs, B. (2008). Discriminating contexts and project management best practices on innovative and non-innovative projects. *Project Management Journal, 39*. S123-S134. doi:10.1002/pmj.20064

Bharath, E. N., Manjula, S. N., & Vijaychand, A. A. (2011). In silico drug design-tool for overcoming the innovation deficit in the drug discovery process. *International Journal of Pharmacy & Pharmaceutical Sciences*, *3*(2), 8-12.

Bhogal, N., & Balls, M. (2008). Translation of new technologies: from basic research to drug discovery and development. *Current Drug Discovery Technologies*, *5*(3), 250-262.

Blake, A. M., & Moseley, J. L. (2011). Frederick Winslow Taylor: one hundred years of managerial insight. *International Journal Of Management, 28*(4), 346-353.

Boell, S. K., & Cecez-Kecmanovic, D. (2010). Literature reviews and the hermeneutic circle. *Australian Academic & Research Libraries*, *41*(2), 129-144.

Boehm, B. (2007). A spiral model of software development and enhancement. Hoboken, NJ: John Wiley and Sons.

Borelli, J. L., Sbarra, D. A., Mehl, M., & David, D. H. (2011). Experiential connectedness in children's attachment interviews: an examination of natural word use. *Personal Relationships, 18*(3), 341-351. doi:10.1111/j.1475-6811.2010.01294.x

Brogan, J. W. (2011). Exonerating Frederial Taylor. *Industrial Engineer: IE, 43*(11), 41.

Cerpa, N., & Verner, J. M. (2009). Why did your project fail? *Communications Of The ACM, 52*(12), 130-134.

Carolina Chamber of Commerce (2012). Biotechnology, pharmaceutical & life sciences companies In North Carolina. Retrieved February 6th, 2012 from http://thrivenc.com/sites/default/files/uploads/Biotechnology_Pharmaceuticals_LifeSciences_Facts.pdf

Civan, A., & Maloney, M. T. (2009). The effect of price on pharmaceutical r&d. b.e. *Journal Of Economic Analysis & Policy: Contributions To Economic Analysis & Policy, 9*(1), 1-22.

Cunningham, R. A. (2011). Douglas McGregor – a lasting impression. *Ivey Business Journal, 75*(5), 5.

Damaré, B. (2008). Workplace learning to improve IT project management. *Public Manager, 37*(4), 45-50. Retrieved from http://search.proquest.com/docview/236317764?accountid=35812

Darmody, P. B. (2007). Henry L. Gantt and Frederick Taylor: the pioneers of scientific management. *AACE International Transactions*, 15.1-15.3.

De Meuse, K. P., Dai, G., & Hallenbeck, G. S. (2010). Learning agility: a construct whose time has come. *Consulting Psychology Journal: Practice And Research, 62*(2), 119-130. doi:10.1037/a0019988

Durante, K., Griskevicius, V., Simpson, J., Cantú, S., & Tybur, J. (2012). Sex ratio and women's career choice: does a scarcity of men lead women to choose briefcase over baby? *Journal of Personality And Social Psychology, 103*(1), 121-134. doi:10.1037/a0027949.

Eckell, D. (2010). Optical solutions for the collocation data center. *Cabling Installation &*

Maintenance, 18(6), 5.

Elo, S., & Kyngas, H. (2008). The qualitative content analysis process. *Journal of Advanced Nursing, 62*(1), 107-115

Edington, B., & Ouellette, B. (2011). Structural capital and project processes: areas for future focus. *Proceedings of The European Conference On Management, Leadership & Governance*, 123-128.

Failure rates finally drop. (2011). *PM Network, 25*(8), 10-11.

Gaobo, P. & Mark , W. (2008). Default investment options in defined contribution plans: A quantitative comparison. *Pension : An International Journal, 13*(4), 221-227.

Gill, D., & Griffin, A. (2010). Good medical practice: what are we trying to say? textual analysis using tag clouds. *Medical Education, 44*(3), 316-322. doi:10.1111/j.1365-2923.2009.03588.x

Graham, A., & Erwin, K. D. (2011). "I Don't Think Black Men Teach Because How They Get Treated as Students": High-Achieving African American Boys' Perceptions of Teaching as a Career Option. *Journal of Negro Education, 80*(3), 398-416.

Gudarzi, G., & Chegin, M. (2011). Using direction finder to evaluate project leadership dimensions case study: iranian project managers. *Interdisciplinary Journal Of Contemporary Research In Business, 2*(12), 966-985.

Hands, K., Peiris, D., & Gregor, P. (2004). Development of a computer-based interviewing tool to enhance the requirements gathering process. *Requirements Engineering*, *9*(3), 204-217. doi:10.1007/s00766-003-0185-x.

Hsieh, C. (2009). Health, quality of care and quality of life: a case of frail older adults. *Social Indicators Research, 94*(1), 61. Retrieved from MasterFILE Premier database.

Hough, A. (2011). 'Disastrous' £11.4bn NHS IT programme to be abandoned. *The Telegraph.* Retrieved from http://www.telegraph.co.uk/health/healthnews/8780566/Disastrous-11.4bn-NHS-IT-programme-to-be-abandoned.html.

Hurt, M., & Thomas, J. L. (2009). Building value through sustainable project management offices. *Project Management Journal, 40*(1), 55-72. doi:10.1002/pmj.20095.

Ionel, N. (2009). Agile software development methodologies: an overview of the current state of research. *Annals of the University of Oradea, Economic Science Series*, *18*(4), 381-385.

Jacquot, J. (2009). Numbers. *Discover*, 30(6), 18.

Jani, A. (2011). Escalation of commitment in troubled IT projects: Influence of project risk factors and self-efficacy on the perception of risk and the commitment to a failing project. *International Journal of Project Management, 29*(7), 934.

Karlsen, J., Andersen, J., Birkely, L. S., & Odega, E. (2005). What characterizes successful it projects. *International Journal of Information Technology & Decision Making*, *4*(4), 525-540.

Kaitin, K. (2010). Deconstructing the drug development process: the new face of innovation. *Clinical Pharmacology And Therapeutics*, *87*(3), 356-361.

Keil, M., & Mähring, M. (2010). Is your project turning into a black hole?. *California Management Review*, *53*(1), 6-31.

Kopelman, R. E., Prottas, D. J., & Davis, A. L. (2008). Douglas McGregor's Theory X and Y: toward a construct-valid measure. *Journal Of Managerial Issues, 20*(2), 255-271.

Leedy, P. D. & Ormrod, J. E. (2010). Practical research: planning and design (9th ed.). UpperSaddle River, NJ: Pearson

Lenfle S, Loch C. (2010). Lost roots: how project management came to emphasize control over flexibility and novelty. *California Management Review* [serial online]. Fall2010 2010;*53*(1):32-55. Available from: Business Source Complete, Ipswich, MA. Accessed August 27, 2011.

Liguo, Y. (2008). Prototyping, domain specific language, and testing. *Engineering Letters*, *17*(1), 6-11.

Lloyd-Walker, B. & Walker, D. (2011). Authentic leadership for 21st century project delivery. *International Journal of Project Management, 29* (European Academy of Management (EURAM 2010) Conference), 383-395. doi:10.1017/j.ijproman.2011.02.004

Lovejoy, T. I., Demireva, P. D., Grayson, J., & McNamara, J. R. (2009). Advancing the practice of online psychotherapy: an application of Rogers' diffusion of innovations theory. *Psychotherapy: Theory, Research, Practice, Training, 46*(1), 112-124. doi:10.1037/a0015153.

Martin, N. L., Pearson, J. M., & Furumo, K. (2007). IS project management: size, practices and the project management office. *Journal of Computer Information Systems, 47*(4), 52–60.

McLean, J. (2011). Fayol - standing the test of time. *Manager: British Journal Of Administrative Management*, (74), 32-33.

Microsoft Corporation. (2006). Testing methodologies. *Microsoft Patterns & Practices*. Retrieved from http://msdn.microsoft.com/en-us/library/ff649520.aspx.

Mikhail, S., & Giddings, R. (2011). Clinical contracting efficiency. *Applied Clinical Trials, 20*(8), 24-31.

Morris, R. A. (2008). Stop the insanity of failing projects. *Industrial Management, 50*(6), 20.

Myers Jr., L. A. (2011). One hundred years later: what would Frederick W. Taylor say?. *International Journal Of Business & Social Science, 2*(20), 8-11.

Nah, F., & Delgado, S. (2006). Critical success factors for enterprise resource planning implementation and upgrade. *Journal of Computer Information Systems*, 4799-113.

Nănău, C. (2010). Automated test generation and agile methodologies. *Bulletin Of The Transilvania University Of Brasov, Series III: Mathematics, Informatics, Physics, 3*(52), 183-190.

Neuman, W. L. (2006). Social research methods: qualitative and quantitative approaches.(6th ed.)Upper Saddle River, NJ: Prentice Hall.

Noffke, T. (2007). No time to delay. *Pharmaceutical Executive, 2722*-27.

Nwachukwu, C. (2010). Living up to information technology's promise: a project management implementation and performance perception. *Interdisciplinary Journal of Contemporary Research in Business, 2*(4), 84-103.

Ojiako, U, Johansen, E., David, G. (2008). A qualitative re-construction of project measurement criteria. *Industrial Management + Data Systems, 108*(3), 405. Retrieved from ProQuest: ABI/INFORM Complete database.

Olson, D. L., & Zhao, F. F. (2007). CIOs' perspectives of critical success factors in ERP upgrade projects. *Enterprise Information Systems*, *1*(1), 129-138. doi:10.1080/17517570601088364.

Ong, V., Richardson, D., Yanqing, D., Qile, H., & Johnson, B. (2009). The role of project leadership in achieving effective project management. *Proceedings of The European Conference on Management, Leadership & Governance*, 157-173.

Oswick, C., Fleming, P., & Hanlon, G. (2011). From borrowing to blending: rethinking the processes of organizational theory building. *Academy of Management Review, 36*(2), 318-337. doi:10.5465/AMR.2011.59330932.

PMI (2009). Project Management Institute's chaos report. New York, NY: PMI

Polit, D. & Beck, C. (2008). *Nursing research: generating and assessing evidence for nursing practice* (8th ed.). Philadelphia, PA: Lippincott Williams & Wilkins

Pollard, C., & Cater-Steel, A. (2009). Justifications, strategies, and critical success factors in successful itil implementations in US and Australian companies: an exploratory study. *Information Systems Management, 26*(2), 174-175. doi:10.1080/10580530902797540.

Popa, M. (2010). Audit process during projects for development of new mobile IT Applications. *Informatica Economica, 14*(3), 34-46.

Pringle, J., Drummond, J., McLafferty, E., & Hendry, C. (2011). Interpretative phenomenological analysis: a discussion and critique. *Nurse Researcher, 18*(3), 20-24.

Project Management Institute (PMI). (2008). A guide to the project management body of knowledge (pmbok guide) – fourth edition. Newtown Square, PA: PMI.

Project zero delay accelerates drug path to clinical trial. (cover story). (2009). *Biotech Business, 22*(9), 1-3.

Pryor. M., & Taneja, S. (2010). Henri Fayol, practitioner and theoretician – revered and reviled. *Journal of Management History, 17*(4), 489-503.

Qumer, A., & Henderson-Sellers, B. (2008). An evaluation of the degree of agility in six agile methods and its applicability for method engineering. *Information and Software Technology, 50*(4), 280-295.

Rivard, S., & Dupré, R. (2009). Information systems project management in pmj: A brief history. *Project Management Journal*, *40*(4), 20-30.

Sandbaek, A. (2006). Qualitative methods used for effect studies and evaluations of healthcare strategies?. *Scandinavian Journal of Primary Health Care*. pp. 131-132.

Scott, J. E., & Vessey, I. (2002). Managing risks in enterprise systems implementations. *Communications of The ACM, 45*(4), 74-81.

Sekhon, B., & Kamboj, S. (2010). Microfluidics technology for drug discovery and development - an overview. *International Journal of PharmTech Research*, 2(1), 804-809.

Shank, G.D. (2006). *Qualitative research: A personal skills approach* (2nd ed.) Upper Saddle River, NJ: Pearson.

Soffer, T., Nachmias, R., & Ram, J. (2010). Diffusion of web supported instruction in higher education - the case of tel-aviv university. *Journal Of Educational Technology & Society,13*(3), 212-223.

Sridhar, S. (2010). Software testing: the old & the new. *Siliconindia*, *13*(10), 26-27.

Stancu, I., & Rece, D. (2010). Embedded banking security level index and aimed control template for banking systems – implementation evaluation using the vroom-yetton-jago contingency model. *Review of Finance & Banking, 2*(2), 77-82.

Standing, T. (2011). Grandmothers' changes in caregiving status. *Virginia Henderson International Nursing Library*. Retrieved from http://www.nursinglibrary.org/vhl/handle/10755/160299

Sweet, L. (2002). Telephone interviewing: Is it compatible with interpretive phenomenological research? *Contemporary Nurse, 12*(1), 58-63.

Tobbell, D. A. (2009). Pharmaceutical networks: the political economy of drug development in the united states, 1945–1980. 10(4), 675-686. doi:10.1093/es/khp039.

Varu, R. K., & Khanna, A. (2010). Opportunities and challenges to implementing quality by design approach in generic drug development. *Journal of Generic Medicines, 7*(1), 60-73. doi:10.1057/jgm.2009.37

WebMD. (2011). Cholesterol management. Retrieved from http://www.webmd.com/cholesterol-management/default.htm

Wee-Kiat, L., Siew Kien, S., & Adrian, Y. (2011). Managing risks in a failing it project: a social constructionist view. *Journal of the Association for Information Systems, 12*(6), 414-440.

Weiyin, H., Thong, J. L., Chasalow, L. C., & Dhillon, G. (2011). User acceptance of agile information systems: a model and empirical test. *Journal of Management Information Systems, 28*(1), 235-272.

Willis, J. W. (2007). Foundations of qualitative research: Interpretive and critical approaches. Thousand Oaks, CA: Sage.

Woo, J., Wolfgang, S., & Batista, H. (2008). The effect of globalization of drug manufacturing, production, and sourcing and challenges for American drug safety. *Clinical Pharmacology and Therapeutics*, 83(3), 494-497.

Wurst, T. A., & Guernsey, B. G. (2006). Drug development on rails. *Applied Clinical Trials, 15*(8), 38-44.

Yang, Y., Onita, C., Xihui, Z., & Dhaliwal, J. (2011). Testqual: conceptualizing software testing as a service. *e-Service Journal, 7*(2), 46-65. doi:10.2979/eservicej.7.2.46.

University of Bremen (2003). Project Management World Study. Retrieved from http://pmi-ber.de/archiv/20050512-greg/pmi.pdf

Appendixes:

Appendix A
Introduction Letter

Dear Participant,

I am a University of Phoenix doctoral student studying organizational leadership and information systems management. My research study, phenomenological analysis of IT project management in pharmaceutical industry, aims to understand why these projects continue to fail at a high rate of 72%. The purpose of this qualitative phenomenological study is to explore the first-hand experiences of stakeholders, project managers, and team members of failed IT projects in the Research Triangle Park, North Carolina area. The study will include an exploration and analysis of the perceptions of the participants on which types of projects and what phases do projects usually fail and why.

Your participation in this study is voluntary. Your discussion during the interview will provide valuable ideas and perspectives on why IT projects failed. The participation will require approximately one hour of your time. You will be anonymous in this research study. Your demographic profile will not be shared with other individuals. I am responsible for keeping your confidentiality and anonymity. I see no adverse risk in your participation for this study; however, you have the right to withdraw at anytime, prior to or during the interview, for any reason without penalty. My study may benefit pharmaceutical organizations by providing the framework for explaining what can be different to increase success chances for IT projects. One indirect benefit to you is to enhance your understanding of project management best practices and methodology.

If you have any questions concerning this research study, please contact me at

PCLY@yahoo.com or 919-368-0914

Sincerely,

Phil Ly

Doctoral Student

University of Phoenix

Participant's Signature_______________________________

Appendix B

UNIVERSITY OF PHOENIX

Informed Consent, Confidentiality Agreement, & Participants 18 years of age and older

Dear Participant,

My name is Phil Ly and I am a student at the University of Phoenix working on a doctorate degree. I am conducting a research study entitled phenomenological analysis of IT project management in pharmaceutical industry. The purpose of the research study is to analyze why IT projects continue to fail at a high rate in the pharmaceutical industry.

Your participation will involve a one hour interview with possible follow-up questions. Your participation in this study is voluntary. If you choose not to participate or to withdraw from the study at any time, you can do so without penalty or loss of benefit to yourself. The results of the research study may be published but your identity will remain confidential and your name will not be disclosed to any outside party.

In this research, there are no foreseeable risks.

Although there may be no direct benefit to you, a possible benefit of your participation is better understanding of what are leading root causes of IT project failures.

If you have any questions concerning the research study, please contact me at PCLY@yahoo.com or 919-368-0914

As a participant in this study, you should understand the following:

1. You may decline to participate or withdraw from participation at any time without consequences.
2. Your identity will be kept confidential.
3. Phil Ly, the researcher, has thoroughly explained the parameters of the research study and all of your questions and concerns have been addressed.
4. If the interviews are recorded, you must grant permission for the researcher, Phil Ly, to digitally record the interview. You understand that the information from the recorded interviews may be transcribed. The researcher will structure a coding process to assure that anonymity of your name is protected.
5. Data will be stored in a secure and locked area. The data will be held for a period of three year, and then destroyed.
6. The research results will be used for publication.

"By signing this form you acknowledge that you understand the nature of the study, the potential risks to you as a participant, and the means by which your identity will be kept confidential. Your signature on this form also indicates that you are 18 years old or older and that you give your permission to voluntarily serve as a participant in the study described with an option to withdraw anytime without penalty of any kind."

Signature of the interviewee ___________________________ Date ___________

Signature of the researcher _____________________________ Date ___________

Appendix C

Interview Questions derived from Research Questions:

Research Questions	Interview Questions
RQ1: What factors cause information technology projects to continue failing at a high rate?	1. At what phase of the project life cycle did you see red flags or failure signs? 2. What are your thoughts on the requirements phase? 3. What are your thoughts on the system development phase? 4. What are your thoughts on the testing phase? 5. What are your thoughts on deployment / implementation phase?
RQ2: What effect does project management software such as Microsoft Project have on project failures?	6. What are your perspectives on the project management tools used in the project? 7. What tools may have been more beneficial to the project?
RQ3: What leadership characteristics do successful project managers have?	8. Describe the characteristics of the project manager for this failed IT project. 9. What did he or she do on the project

	that you thought were great? 10. What did he or she do on the project that was terrible?
RQ4: What effect does PMI training and certification of project managers have on failure experiences?	11. From your perspective, please rate the experience level of the project manager on the failed IT project. 12. What kind of project management best practices did they use throughout the project?
Demographics	1. Role 2. Years of Professional Experience 3. Education 4. Gender

Appendix D

Permission to use Premise:

UNIVERSITY OF PHOENIX

PERMISSION TO USE PREMISES, NAME, AND/OR SUBJECTS

at

Wake County Cary Library

Name of Facility, Organization, University, Institution, or Association

Check any that apply:

☑ I hereby authorize Phil Ly, student of University of Phoenix, to use the premises (facility identified below) to conduct a study Qualitative Phenomenological Analysis of IT Project Management in Pharmaceutical Industry.

☐ I hereby authorize Phil Ly, student of University of Phoenix, to recruit subjects for participation in conducting a study entitled Qualitative Phenomenological Analysis of IT Project Management in Pharmaceutical Industry.

☑ I hereby authorize Phil Ly, student of University of Phoenix, to use the name of the facility, organization, university, institution, or association identified above when publishing results from the study entitled Qualitative Phenomenological Analysis of IT Project Management in Pharmaceutical Industry.

[signature] 5 / 2 / 12

Signature Date

Elizabeth Bartlett

Name

Branch Manager

Title

310 South Academy Street, Cary, NC, 27511 Phone: (919) 460-3350

Address of Facility

1

UNIVERSITY OF PHOENIX

PERMISSION TO USE PREMISES, NAME, AND/OR SUBJECTS

at

The Project Management Institute North Carolina Chapter

Check any that apply:

☒ I hereby authorize Phil Ly, student of University of Phoenix, to post a Power Point slide of one (1) page, which the Chapter may edit, to be submitted to the President by close of business (eastern day light time) by May 11, 2012, in the rotating slide deck before the May Chapter Meeting to solicit participants to contact Phil directly in order to conduct a survey related to the study of Qualitative Phenomenological Analysis of IT Project Management In Pharmaceutical Industry.

Robert Matan 5/2/2012

Signature Date

/s/ Robert Matan

Name

President, The Project Management Institute North Carolina Chapter

Title

Appendix E

Interview Summary Data of Participants by Research Questions

RQ1: What factors cause information technology projects to continue failing at a high rate?	
At what phase of the project life cycle did you see red flags or failure signs?	Planning phase. Requirements not clear. Not organized. Execution will confirm failure. Defining the project.
	Often very early on, in the planning phase. Lack of understanding the business, cultural and time zone issues cause project failures.
	Planning - Lack of resources or skilled resources.
	12 years of project management, red flags right at approval because the organization wants project sooner than planned out to take. Ripple effect from there. Domino effect.
	Early on project, when resources were not available to deliver implementation. Early stage milestones were already missed… simple

	ones.
	Most of projects fail when capacity is reached. No future growth for capacity.
	Happens at pre-launch, don't fully understand cost and life-cycle. Has a project plan but sustainability for support is under-value.
	Early in development, first started in development. The Requirements were not stable. 12 messages passed, but no agreement on any of them. Cobalt coding days, this field is that, is like mapping data from one database to another. XML. Database 1 did not talk to Database 2. Dept of how bad unfolded over time.
	Requirements phase because requirements poorly defined. Little cooperation. Changing requirements.

	Basically, can sense problem before reporting. Requirements phase when discussing time line and scope. Challenging project in tight time line raises flags, But issues not raised until later in reporting. Flags are raised formally during risks and issue reporting, but gut feeling was problem long before reporting.
	Very beginning. Definition of concept phase. Ideas being discussed.
	Scoping, even before requirements, red flags around sponsorship, ownership, and change analysis. Business and system requirements do not match.
	Diagnose phase or requirements gathering phase.
	During implementation, The project had 12

	phases. The previous Project Manager took 2 years. Current Project Manager took 1 year. Implementation piece failed for only one of twelve phases.
	Design phase shows red flags. Inability to produce to specification. Skip over, avoid decisions till later.
What are your thoughts on the requirements phase?	Scoping an issue. Process for collecting requirements very loose. Very general discussion. Two end of spectrum. Not specific enough. Don't understand magnitude. People can "build" the requirements.
	It will always be difficult for the business to speak IT talk, and IT to understand business speak.
	Requirements are a major component of a successful project. Requirements need to be clearly defined and agreed with stakeholders.

	Projects that do not take time to do requirements. No proof of concept. People do not see what they will get. Doom to fail.
	The scope of functionality is not well understood. Hard to nail down requirements when you don't know what end result should be. Sizing, similar to scope, again what is the total size of implementation. How many people, systems, and processes.
	Inefficient data to project how much space and memory are correctly estimated in requirements. Requirements do not know how many users will use systems. Lack of data to complete requirements.
	Typical phrase, give customers what they asked for but not what they needed. Tough communications battle. Therefore, delivery is

	granular than what is delivered. We missed the actual business requirements. We think about features and functions but actually forget about the business requirements.
	No sign-off on requirements and no agreed change control process. We did not realize but project leadership did not have control in place to get people sending data, transporting data, to receiving data to agree on design specs. The pieces were destined to fail. Gravel truck containing oil will not go.
	Requirements phase because requirements poorly defined. Little cooperation.
	Common problem is requirements too high level and unclear and difficult to measure success. Not detailed enough.
	Scope not well defined, do not know all

	requirements. Requirements not complete. Person defining did not have full scope or accountability, did not think through, do not have authority to define requirements. One additional is process changes and use cases defined or understood. Lack of scenario modeling. Use case understanding.
	Don't know who intended customers are, so do not know what they want. Don't understand business process to support.
	Basically, no formal agreement on scope, in fighting on what requirements meant or did mean. No clarity on outcome and benefits based on those requirements.
	Requirements failure, to get job done, without enough direction from management and without proper oversight from management.
	Where most projects go wrong. Reason is we

	don't fully understand problems we are trying to solve. Creating requirements really don't drive biggest benefits or address underlying issues that project is based of. Address every single requirement rather than most important requirements.
What are your thoughts on the system development phase?	Requirements not clear will lead to poor development. Coders do not understand requirements. Development not to specification. You know, estimation is off regardless waterfall or agile. Skill set of estimation not good.
	Smaller iterations of work lead to better results.
	You need to have competent developers who can develop to the requirements and should have iterative reviews with stakeholders to ensure development expectations are met.

	Not delivering smaller pieces, code something for very long time and no visibility right away and too far down the path that went of tangent. Offshoring development is less successful translating requirements to development. Language, cultural, and time barriers. Even more challenging to deliver something to meet expectations. Often get requirements that are just functional or business requirements that come from other areas such as IT security and risk areas and maybe aren't in purview of developers at the time and may miss those requirements. Security risks that needed to be addressed.
	Scope creep is the biggest problem. Clear requirements, scope creep, incorrect assumptions.
	Most of the time, development conducted on requirements. So when requirements are

	wrong, development codes are wrong.
	We think that we miss translating from business requirements into system requirements. We lose sight of the systems and lose track of what business value we are trying to deliver. Lost in translation. Tendency to over-customer, or over-engineer.
	During system development, we were too patient with customers and re-develop our part of the applications over and over again. At some point, we need to lock down. Like closet moving from room to room during house construction. Development lead did not lock down on system requirements, so developers kept looping over same design over and over again.
	A lot of third parties. One major issue was communication, so many layers of

	communications. People talk to many other people before getting to the source. Lost in translation.
	Hmm, think is to do with unclear requirements leading to design. Inexperienced developers working on development.
	Usually breakdown of understanding of requirements and misinterpretation of requirements into development. Lost in translations. Designer or Programmer did not understand because too vague. Lack of completeness. Designer over cover 90 of 100 requirements because forgot or lazy.
	Once we get here, we are mostly fine. Design spec need to trace back to requirements for coders to be effective.
	In fighting of design and what is a good

	design. Because people are not sure in scope. Fracturing between internal and external third party. No common, consistent goals. Individual and unit specific.
	The fact that human being typing in command instead of having commands automated in script beforehand. Trying to remember what to do at midnight because humans make errors.
	Design phase shows red flags. Inability to produce to specification. Skip over, avoid decisions till later. Point is designing on the fly. Which can be okay, if that is intent on how to run projects.
What are your thoughts on the testing phase?	Test strategy is not fit for purpose. Test cases are too easy or will always fail. QA does not understand requirements in the first place. Test teams may write test criteria not based on requirements.

	Dependent upon the size of the work, testing scripts may not be necessary. Larger projects mandate testing scripts.
	Developers must unit test and a QA team must thoroughly system and regression test and report results.
	Simulating production environment. Full-system testing, making sure we have right test cases that we test against everything that the system will do against requirements to fully cover. Making change to existing system, regression testing missed what the change effected the system, something new introduced and caused failure. Load testing – biggest challenge of all to simulate production load. Failed on enterprise applications launched.
	Tests don't test the right thing. Tests don't show that you got a problem. Not testing the right thing. Another common problem is

	testing for low probability issue.
	Lack of testing scenarios. Developers do testing and test only what they know. Will not test all scenarios that users will see.
	We have tendency to under invest in load and performance testing particularly for global applications. Do not invest enough, we pay through re-development or new infrastructure. Back to the budget table.
	Waited for big bang testing, should have tested per deliverable or per functionality. Should have tested little pieces as we went. Real database schema withheld from us as in no testing place or sandbox. Database design in test environment did not match design requirements. We finally got tested in Dev, and moved to QA, we forgot to tell you that schema between Dev and QA did not match.

	Truth of matter is still coding during test.
	Testing connections were not end to end. Only tested new code but not hardware or network of test systems. Cable and network lines too long or too short. Cannot test load, for example 100,000 employees.
	Often testing gets squeezed because of problems up front. Requirements, design issues, addressed in testing, but perception is testing time is not long enough and more testing resources. Previous problems should have been addressed before testing.
	Lack of structure Lack of test plan. No clear test cases that trace back to requirements in design. Rigor around follow-through testing requirements and design components. Test cases expectations not met.

	System and regression testing are average. User testing is below average. Don't know who users are, so test cases do not match to requirements.
	Testing should be first, then develop requirements. No visual performance metrics on how well testing went. No end users involvement. No action plans to address bugs prior to release.
	Not enough testing done. Incorporated large amount of testing to make sure testing is not reason for failing again.
	Often find points back to poor requirements. See we basically instead of test requirements, we write new requirements for testing. Obviously, testing is where people try to recover back project time. Go against testing function, expected to find defects.

What are your thoughts on deployment / implementation phase?	Environment not ready for deployment. Knowing technical requirements. Pre-req not done. How wide is the deployment, nobody knows for sure. Lack of training.
	This is where the business often learns that the requirements were not understood.
	The deployment plan must be reviewed with stakeholders and the production support team and a transition support plan must be in place.
	Lack of communications and coordination. Did not inspect hardware prior to launch. Lack of project documentation to provide to support. Quality issues because of lack of support knowledge.
	Unrealistic schedules. Lack of planning for unforeseen issues.
	It should not have too many problems by deployment. Problems come up after users start using the live systems.
	Actually, good at this, scheduling and impact assessment. Making sure people are ready,

	good job in communications. Training to generic for real business specific content. Here is how the things work instead of solving business issue. Too generic. Product can be better received if training is business specific. What business problem is this solving.
	Project was canned at that point, Out of money, out of time. Pieces did not fit. Ultimately, you got three way breakdown between 3 project management teams. No centralized project management.
	Production rollout did not consider external customers. For example, someone logging in from home or off-site.
	Often, lack of documentation, and documentation not produced up front for deployment. Example, deployment plan and support plan. No testing of deployment. Not enough time to commit to deployment. In addition, deployment team is in different organization and do not get engaged on a

	project till late.
	Lack of control in production env. Updating codes lack of process. Not everything updated. Poor configuration management. Changes not considered during coding.
	Horrible. Do not begin with end in mind. Unsupportable, non user friendly systems. Pockets of people who expect project manager to support system too.
	Need quality test environment. Just throw it in and see what happens. Focus on coding and not support ie. Help Desk to ensure smooth implementation.
	Lack of planning, insufficient testing.
	Users and support are not ready for change in organization. No plan typically has been made to decommission or retire asset to be replaced when that is the case.
RQ2: What effect does project management software such as Microsoft Project have on project failures?	
What are your perspectives on the project management tools used in the project?	Tools have very little impact to project failure. People and process gaps are the main reasons. MS Project, Primavera, Open-source tools.

	Use the tools that match project team. Depend on size of project.
	MS Project is often difficult for the new PM to understand. Training on the tools used are critical for the PM.
	Having a project plan is more important then a specific project plan tool. Having a plan in place that is agreed with stakeholders and team members is necessary.
	Not so much tools, but usage of tools. Successful projects use MS project or excel or visio. Mainly communications, where we are based on schedule, resources, issues, budget, know point in time where we are. Communicate that information to others such as project team and stakeholders.
	MS Project, Primavera, Excel spreadsheets.

	Clarity.
	MS Project. Excel.
	MS Project, Excel good at capturing tasks and time line, Gannt Chart. Vaccum or insolation, task A mistranslated. Regroup on business value. Including some testing along. Agile methodology. Users testing is embedded in the project. Perhaps tools can be engineered tracing back to business requirements. Support would like to see projects coming into support. For satisfied user base to know pipeline. How to ramp up for multiple projects coming at once. Also, relate to business impact of portfolio and strategy across the portfolio. New products and what is impact of getting rid of old one. Plan for known bad value.
	Informal Excel charts and emails.

	MS Project very important.
	MS Project, MS suite of office, risks and issues log (RAID) risks, actions, issues, and dependency. In addition, project tracking for finance. Finance tracking software. In addition, testing tools like quality center. Approval process tools (who approves what, when). Document management tool. Configuration management tool. Change control tool.
	Work breakdown structure, GANTT chart, RACI, process flows, MS Project, risks and issues logs. Status updates.
	Tools are fine. People's education on tool could improve. Use tools for intended purpose such as relationship track, critical path, resourcing. Otherwise, it just be one long excel list. Failure on reporting on project

	progress. Failure on requirements matching. Tools need to be efficient and useful.
	Charter to, baseline plan (MS Project), document to traceability. For example, change scope in charter. Excel to manage risks and issues.
	MS Project, MS Excel, Word, Color graphics tools, simplification – easy for audience. Risks highlighter.
	Active Risk, Assumptions, Issues, Dependency (RAID) tool would be nice. MS Project, but people do not know how to use. Get in way of running projects.
What tools may have been more beneficial to the project?	Social networking type of tools. Collaboration tool like Facebook or Yammer. Community to communicate.
	MS Project is a great tool when fully

	understood by the PM. MS CPC/Sharepoint also is a great tool.
	MS Project is most important for the project manager. Find that sharing a plan is sometimes more beneficial using Word, Excel, PowerPoint and charts.
	MS Project to map project out and resource it. But not most effective tool to communicate with. Something to schedule and resource understand critical path.
	MS Project works fine. Not fault of tool.
	MS Project.
	Missing most is portfolio view of multiple projects. Some tool to give portfolio view.
	MS Project or project-like facility to track time and resources and progress-to-date. Tool permits looping.
	MS Project very important. Linking between project plans from different third party. Cost

	distribution / splitting tool. For example, Contractor A works 50% for this group and 50% for another group. How do we split cost in a project planning. External linkage tools.
	Change control type of tool.
	Traceability tool. Define requirements, design, test cases, testing. Trace everything together. Specific requirements all the way down to code.
	Requirements management and dashboard reporting. Risk register.
	MS Project with leveraging its full features. Use Risks and Issues
	Proper project communication tool.
	RAID Log is very effective when used well.
RQ3: What leadership characteristics do successful project managers have?	
Describe the characteristics of the project manager for this failed IT	Lack of experience. Inflexible. Not people friendly; not work well with others. Soft skills

project.	not there.
	Lack of leadership, unwilling to hold collaborative meetings, discuss all view points. Mostly took a "command and control" attitude.
	Successful project managers must have a project plan in place that is agreed with stakeholders and team members and must be proactive in managing to the plan and anticipating risks. A PM must communicate good and bad news, on a regular basis to stakeholders and team members.
	To be most successful in leading project to communicate benefits, risks, and negotiate timeline cost and quality. Influencing skills. Lack of these led to failure. Stand better chances.
	They did not understand critical path of project. Therefore, effort expended on low-

	value activities. Key ingredient of bad project manager is someone who does not communicate and manage issues well.
	Mostly, the project managers were not organized. Not defining steps correctly. Lack of experience.
	Focus on time and budget, and not focus on quality. Project Manager unaware of other projects with same due dates.
	Former Java programmer promoted to Project Management. Focusing on technology not time, money, and people.
	Not well organized. Not prepared to discuss. Different versions of the truth. Lack of responsibility. Did not push back on scope creep.

	Biggest root cause is probably lack of project management experience.
	Lack of accountability to success of project. Lack of structure, Lack of experience. Lack of methodology. Not consistent in approach.
	Not understanding critical path. Not managing sponsors to remove barriers. Not understanding project well enough to make judgment calls on what is critical versus optional.
	Not well verse in skills and behaviors of project manager, not competent, lack interpersonal and soft skills, not good at conflict management, poor communications skills
	First time project manager doing it, don't know what questions to ask, management did not

	provide oversight.
	Disorganized, too accommodating, too cautious in escalation management. Worry about reflection of escalation as negative. Picking arbitrary dates. Reactive.
What did he or she do on the project that you thought were great?	Nuts and bolts pretty good. Nice project schedule, but not communicate well. PM basics done well.
	Gave folks credit and acknowledgement when the work was done well. Positive attitude, encouragement and bricolage.
	In addition to having an agreed plan, a successful PM must build relationships and develop trust with team members and stakeholders.
	To be able to manage risks and changes and communicate agreement for them. And reset

	baseline with effective change management.
	Driving execution of tasks, tasks management. Typically a project manager will drive people hard on what is written on plan regardless right thing to do or not. People who can re-order the work, so not stuck doing nothing. Proper risk analysis and risk management.
	Communication was constant. Documentation was good.
	Seen very good business change management. Touching base with customers on how features developed or not. Solutions were delivered and expectations already built in. Good stakeholder management. Fix issues with training because of translations between business and system requirements. Set expectations.

	Need to tighten up our process. Six month re-design of processes. Strong lessons-learned from failure.
	Communication and planning. Strategy sessions. Future planning.
	Good intention, good commitment, want to be successful.
	Good Communications. Basically, don't know.
	Tenacity. They tried hard, but end of day, problem was not resolved, and sponsors did not assist.
	Realize when they were in trouble and sought outside help. Maintain current relationships without burning bridges.

	Regularly held all-hands meetings, relationship building. Stakeholder management
	Drove and actively manage the plan. Did the job. Saw themselves as more than keeper of project plan, but owner of outcome of project. Project managers to pressure test people's work.
What did he or she do on the project that was terrible?	Do not listen. No risk management. Cannot fix issues.
	Took credit for the work of the team.
	A PM cannot avoid problems or issues and must be able to find solutions or lead the team to find solutions to problems.
	Numbers of projects that go on in space, one project manager responsible for whole program and do not dependency with other projects.

	Not managing dependency as key failure. Reactive to situation instead of proactive.
	Ignored red flags regarding quality and compliance. Probably did not communicate significant schedule slippages. Not proactively analyzing or managing risks.
	Can't think of anything terrible.
	Worst ones were ignored risks and kept pushing. Frustration from unsatisfied from not mitigating risks. Focus on time and budget but not on actual quality of deliverables.
	Some people wanted the project to fail. PM lost confidence. Could have raised flag, but did not.
	Approval of vacations before important milestone due dates.
	Did not push back what was given to them. For example, unrealistic requirements, unrealistic timelines, don't have enough people. Did not push back on management.

	Lack of accountability.
	Did not listen and take time to understand to make better judgment. Scope creep needs to be kept in check.
	Continue repeat same mistakes to detriment of project. For example, continue to renegotiate deadlines to give resources more time.
	Lack of resources, lack of sufficient subject matter experts (SME).
	Bury issues. Did not seek outside help.
RQ4: What effect does PMI training and certification of project managers have on failure experiences?	
From your perspective, please rate the experience level of the project manager on the failed IT project.	Pick Experience Project managers over rookie. Certifications with experience won over experience only.
	Very little experience
	Find that new and inexperience project

	managers have a higher rate of failure.
	Variation brand new project managers with little training. No PM is immune to project failure regardless of experience level or training.
	Take experience project manager with experience. If experience is equal, take project manager with certifications.
	Would pick years of experience over certifications. If years of experience are similar, then pick training and certifications.
	Inexperience project management. Would pick 20 years experience over academic. If years experience are equal, would pick the PM with more certifications.
	Project was Java developer got promoted to

	Project Manager. No evidence of formal project management training. Would go with 20 years project management experience. If experience is equal, certifications would aid in decision.
	Project management training and certifications are important if they have experience.
	Many project managers seem to understand project management and can manage plan and progress, but lack ability to detect risks and issues. Unable to prevent risks from becoming issues. Like driving a car, but do not know bomb is around the corner because cannot see. Certifications have no correlation to project success. It is about soft skills and experience of the project manager. 20 years experience over certifications with little experience.
	Limited experience on projects. Not PMI PMP certified. But PMP Project Managers do not

	translate to success either.
	Experience wins over certification. Managing people and personal skills come from experience. Need better leadership.
	Amateur. No certifications. Risen up from technical background, not project management background
	Prefer project manager with experience. But if experience being equal, formal training and certification preferred.
	Experience project management experience but no formal training. Few years of experience.
What kind of project management best practices did they use throughout the project?	Great job of scoping and planning and communication. Alignment on expectations. Connecting the dots across the organization. Executive sponsorship actually support and

	backup the project manager.
	a) Solid PM skills using the PMI methodology keeps the project on track, for budget and deliverables. b) Soft skills, keeps the teams at peace and working well together.
	Find that following the PMI methodology is key to a successful project.
	Using best practices from PMI PMBok, right communication, risks and issues management, even if project failed, project was better, failure more accepted.
	Clearly demonstrated path analysis. That guarantee focusing of energy on right stuff at the right time. Having fully resource loaded plan, fully command.
	Good documentation skills. Good

	communication to project team.
	Weekly status reports, business change management and communications along the project.
	Weekly status reports or meetings would be good.
	Strategy meetings to discuss new technologies.
	Lessons learned on why projects failed. Help project manager and team to be better next time.
	Clear scope, strong sponsorship, strong project methodology, commitment, escalation, mitigate risks. Focus on beginning, team members commitment. Write clear requirements.
	Quick notification of risks and issues and follow-up and follow-through. Escalation. Pushing back on scope creep. Ex. need more money or scope if customers want additional features.

	Conducted weekly status meetings, attempted to use MS project, did some stakeholder management.
	Appropriate view, people need to be totally understood. Set expectations and clarify on objectives. With communications across the board.
	Status reporting.

www.ingramcontent.com/pod-product-compliance
Lightning Source LLC
LaVergne TN
LVHW061203120826
845149LV00011B/1886
9781303428333